D1087578

THE
COLONIAL HISTORY
SERIES

General Editor
D. H. Simpson

Librarian of the Royal Commonwealth Society

AFRICAN BLOCKADE

Other titles in this series:

Bridge, Horatio. *Journal of an African Cruiser*, 1845. New introduction by D. H. Simpson.
Reprinted 1968 £2 10

Colomb, Captain. *R.N. Slave Catching in the Indian Ocean*, 1873. A Record of Naval Experiences.
Reprinted 1968 £6 6

Devereux, W. C. *A Cruise in the Gorgon*, 1869. New introduction by D. H. Simpson.
Reprinted 1968 £6 6

Trollope, Anthony. *West Indies and the Spanish Main.* 4th edition 1860. Reprinted 1968. £4

382.44
F742sr
WITHDRAWN

SIX MONTHS' SERVICE

IN THE

AFRICAN BLOCKADE,

FROM

APRIL TO OCTOBER, 1848,

IN COMMAND OF

H.M.S. BONETTA.

BY

LIEUTENANT FORBES, R.N.,

AUTHOR OF "FIVE YEARS IN CHINA."

1969
DAWSONS OF PALL MALL
London

First published in London 1849
Reprinted 1969

Dawsons of Pall Mall
16 Pall Mall, London, S.W.1

SBN 7129 0349 6

Printed in Great Britain
by Photolithography
Unwin Brothers Limited
Woking and London

CONTENTS.

CAT Sep 28 '70

181647

INTRODUCTION.

ALTHOUGH H.M.S. Bonetta has been only six months on the coast of Africa, it must not be imagined that this Work has been composed merely from the experience of so short a service.

In order to give it a freshness, recent scenes and captures are indeed detailed, but the opinions contained in this volume, have been formed from a long series of service, viz.—of nine years in the West Indies; a voyage of four months in a slave ship (one of many captured) from Cuba to Bermuda; and another across the Atlantic to Sierra Leone, in 1838.

The Slave Trade is a vast speculation. The vast gains attending this traffic are scarcely conceivable, and, from the great number of vessels fitted for the purpose, most certain. The profitable result is pretty well calculated by the merchant;

and although it is a lottery to the people employed, he is safe enough. He fits out four, and expects to lose three vessels; if he should lose only two, he would consider himself lucky.

Captures are, therefore, really of small consequence to the Slave-merchant, and certainly of little use towards the suppression or extinction of the Trade. During twenty-six years, 103,000 slaves have been emancipated; while in the same period 1,795,000 slaves were actually landed! or rather more than over 69,000 slaves annually! (See Parliamentary Reports), and last year (notwithstanding the enormous proportion of empty vessels taken), 60,000 slaves were landed!!

On the other hand, the shipment is generally by agency, the merchant on the coast receiving bills to an enormous amount, payable only in the event of the vessel arriving in port. He is content to bear the loss should she be taken, because one cargo in six will pay him well. As a proof how much must be gained by this system, slaves were sold on the coast of Africa in 1847, for a mere song,—an old musket was considered too much,—while in the Brazils they realized *50l.* a-piece.

So long as there is a demand there will be slavers. No native Government will declare the Trade piracy, though it be carried on as such, and even suppose they did, the Trade would only be checked, and perhaps stopped for a time, but then the price of labour in the Brazils would increase so much in consequence of the demand, that the moment the blockade was raised, hundreds would risk even a pirate's doom.

Burn and destroy wherever the merchant places his factory, and ruin must follow; but relax vigilance and his successor will re-commence.

There is only one real cure for the Slave Trade, and that is the introduction of a cheap and useful system of Trade under Government superintendance, assisted by a reduction of prices at first, but no presents. Returns for a length of time would be necessarily small, but large quantities of palm and ground-nut oil, camwood and ivory, might soon be brought into the market.

A naturally indolent people are not to be made industrious in a day or a year; but once open a market, and the whole state of society may be altered. The liberated African at Sierra Leone is a good example.

Africa being by no means over-populated, labour would soon rise in demand, and the people becoming civilized, would train their offspring to the management of agricultural implements, instead of warlike weapons, which, having no longer use for them, would be laid aside.

So vast a change cannot be effected for a long time to come; in the meantime emigration might be promoted, which, subject to authority, could be easily managed.

Allowing that the Slave Trade would still be carried on for some years to come, it is not to be supposed that more than 60,000 yearly would be smuggled, exclusive of emigrants. The horrors of the transatlantic voyage, however, would be much alleviated by the raising of the blockade, there would be no fear of capture, and then the merchant would secure all the vessels he fitted out, and consequently be able to make a more liberal allowance of room and food to the slave.

For some time, no doubt, the practice of selling slaves would continue; but, as the legitimate Trade increased, the other would diminish; while the shipper, being no longer afraid of losses, would purchase according to the demand; and not fill his barracoons with all that were offered, sometimes with a chance of starving them, because he cannot supply the necessary amount of food.

Treaties might then be enforced if they were broken; while now, to expect an African king to keep a treaty, and offer him nothing but a dazzling present—to do this is idle. It is only placing him at the tender mercies of his subjects, who, assisted by Slave-merchants, would assuredly murder him.

The scenes and captures, described in this Work, are from a service, now ended, on the northern division of the Blockade, which is divided into three stations, the other two being the Bights of Benin and Biafra, and the South Coast.

January, 1849.

AFRICAN BLOCKADE.

CHAPTER I.

THE VOYAGE OUT.

LEAVING Plymouth, in the middle of January, 1848, the Bonetta was nearly torn to pieces, when, carrying the mails for St. Michael's, she cast anchor in Delgada Bay. Scarcely had the boat reached the shore, than, at the recommendation of the inhabitants, she returned. The sea was rolling in with great violence from the southward, indicating a gale from that quarter, which, before noon, had so increased, that, in company with twenty-five sail of fruit-traders, and leaving an anchor and cable behind, sail was made, and with difficulty she was beat out of the bay.

A word of the St. Michael's trade in oranges. The time of the year, both in the Island and Great Britain, is the most dangerous; the cargo perishable, and the vessels, though beautiful, very small: and lucky are they if the southerly gales do not drive them from their anchorage more than once.

With what hospitality were we received at Madeira! all that might be said in the present work, would be but a repetition of what has been so often and truly described.

Honoured by the presence of Her Majesty the Queen Dowager of England, the Crown-Prince of Holland, the Dukes of Saxe Weimar and Palmella, besides a host of nobility, balls, parties, and picnics were the order of the day.

Leaving Madeira, it was our fate to behold one of the most extraordinary contrasts; Madeira, the beautiful and cultivated—Bona Vista, nothing but a mass of sand and stone.

This was the dry season, and not a blade of grass, or a patch of verdure, was visible; a mist hung over the land, which; if that were possible, added to the dreariness of its appearance: yet, some little time since, this was a fashionable, and was considered a healthy resort: the Governor-General of the Cape de Verdes, all the foreign consuls, and the Mixed Commission Court, resided here,—several ladies spread a grace over the society; and, visited by French, American, and English men-of-war, Bona Vista was, at least, a happy place.

One of those terrible visitations, so difficult to account for, in one fell swoop almost depopulated the island. Its cause has raised a controversy among medical men; even the animals fell victims, and upwards of a hundred horses died.

The only Europeans at present on the island are the Governor a Portuguese colonel, the Alfarez in charge of the detachment of troops, and an Englishman, a sort of consular agent.

Bona Vista produces nothing but salt, and its inhabitants get their supplies of commodities from the neighbouring islands.

Whalers frequently call here to refit, and the immorality of the inhabitants is considerably increased by intercourse with the sailors. In this town almost every other house is a grog-shop, of the lowest conceivable order, in which liquors of the worst possible kind are retailed.

While we lay there, a most desperate attempt at murder was perpetrated. The only limbs of the law, the judge and clerk of the court, were both natives. A miscreant, arraigned for theft, was no sooner sentenced to banishment to a still more miserable island of the same group, than, drawing his knife, he suceeeded in stabbing the judge three successive times, and the clerk once, before he was secured.

As a chapter will be devoted to Sierra Leone, suffice it now to say, that the mails being duly landed, the Bonetta proceeded on her way, and coasting down afforded a pleasant opportunity of enjoying a most delightful voyage to Kobenda.

From Sierra Leone certain shoals, called the St. Anne's, prevent a close inspection of the scenery about the mouths of the Sherboro and Sherbro rivers.

Between these and Cape Mount, nothing picturesque meets the eye. A long sandy beach, topped by here and there a row of palm or other trees, and now and then a vacancy shewing the entrance of a river, offers too much sameness to be pleasing. Cape Mount, rising about twelve hundred feet above the level of the sea, and covered with a verdant forest, is, indeed, a pleasant contrast, while, on a clear day, a continuity of hill can be traced, which is known to be beyond the ken of the white man, and is consequently gazed upon with curiosity.

Between Cape Mount and Cape Palmas, the coast is very irregular; but generally with beautiful blue hills in the back ground, which offer a pleasant relief to the ever-verdant appearance of the nearer shores.

On the 14th of March, at daylight, we were in sight of the beautiful little island of Annobon, nominally a colony of the Portuguese.

The inhabitants are said to be descended from the slaves of a Portuguese slave-ship, which was wrecked on these shores many years ago: they are intelligent and industrious. Their frequent intercourse with ships has enabled them to speak French, Portuguese, Spanish, English, and several African languages. The produce of their industry is brought off to all vessels passing, and exchanged for old clothes, &c. The number of inhabitants is said to be 3,000.

About three years since, one of the most heinous crimes that ever disgraced humanity, was committed by the captain of a Spanish slave-vessel, on these confiding islanders.

Touching at Annobon for water, on a voyage from Cuba to Africa, the captain was much pleased with the industrious habits of the islanders. Having employed a large number on his vessel, he invited them to bring their friends on the day they were to receive payment; accordingly, hundreds being on his decks, and more in canoes, part of the sailors beat those on board below, while the rest in boats captured the canoes. In this way he sailed for the Havannah, with a cargo of 4 or 500 slaves.

Running into the anchorage, the captain of the Dois Amigos, a Brazilian prize to H. M. S. Bonetta, drew my attention to the circumstance that the flag was not hoisted, and then he told me the above tale, stating that until they were certain of the vessel not being a Spaniard, no canoe would leave the shore.

Scarcely were we within three miles, when dozens of canoes surrounded us, and the crews gaining confidence, soon crowded the decks, when a brisk barter ensued.

During the afternoon, a smartly-dressed black made his appearance. He was habited in a flowing coat of green and red baize, trimmed with yellow braid, knee inexpressibles, and purser's hose and shoes. The costume had evidently been invented by some marine tailor on board one of H. M. ships. This personage was attended by two followers, one of whom he described as his mate. Descending below, he asked for all he saw, and was dismissed in a state of inebriety from the officers' mess, for secreting a tumbler (after drinking the contents) under his royal robes. This was the King, as he himself told us:—"I King dis country." He corroborated the truth of the story of the Spanish slaver, with sundry oaths and curses.

The island is extremely productive, and abounds in most delicious fresh water. On the top of the hill, which may be said to rise from the base on all sides, is a fresh-water lake, in some parts four and five fathoms deep. Annobon has a healthy appearance, although report asserts that appearances are not always to be relied upon.

The coast about Malemba Bay is certainly most beautiful, and is compared by many to the land about Cornwall. It consists of park scenery, backed by ranges of forest hills. Malemba Bay is much like Mount Edgecombe. At Kobenda Bay, which is situated to the northward of the Congo River, we found H. M. S. Penelope, bearing the pendant of the Commander-in-Chief, and from him we received orders to proceed to Ascension.

This bay and Malemba are both frequented by the slave-vessels; and at the town, bearing the name of the former, are several factories. The town is large, and built on rising ground: there we landed thirty-six prisoners, the crew of a slaver taken on the voyage, with 408 slaves on board—but of that in its place.

On arriving at Ascension, our outward voyage may be said to have ended. Everybody is aware that there is such an island, and that it is garrisoned by marines, and governed by a captain in Her Majesty's Navy; but everybody may not be aware of the essential value, and the actual necessity (so long as the African squadron be kept up), of the considerable disbursement required for its support. Yet, such is the case; and without Ascension, or a healthy spot, far removed from the coast malaria, our losses from fever, though now severe, would be considerably increased.

CHAPTER II.

SIERRA LEONE.

THE most ill-built town in the British colonies, with the most picturesque natural position, may be said to be Freetown, the capital of Sierra Leone. It is by no means necessary, in the present work, to point out to the reader that the church wanted white-washing, to render it respectable, &c., or to describe other public buildings; but there are two it may be as well to mention. These are the Liberated African Establishment and the Hospital. In the former, the emancipated negroes are placed on landing, and every comfort they can require is granted to them; while those under medical treatment are received in the latter.

Formerly, the younger were bound apprentices for periods, varying from two to five years, to any resident who would pay one pound for indentures, and become responsible for the maintenance, clothing, and education of the apprentice. Adults received besides, an outfit of farm utensils, and twopence daily for six months; they were located in the different villages, but as, at the end of that time, they were worse off, generally speaking, than at the commencement, the entire system underwent a change. The apprenticeship-system was put an end to, and children were received into the various schools, and an emigration was opened to the West Indies, of which many of both sexes took advantage; the remainder either enlisted in one or the other of the West Indian corps, which are entirely recruited from this source, or were located in villages among people of their own tribes, who received them into their families, and, after a short period of labour, started them in the world as the possessors of small huts. This was, and is the general practice, but many follow trades, and some enter as sailors on board men-of-war and merchant ships.

The trades are often only half learnt: a carpenter was required on board the Bonetta, and one of the liberated Africans offered himself; the ship's carpenter examined him, and pronounced him a capital hand, and that he could use the adze well. He obtained leave to the day the ship left. The following morning, at sea, the carpenter appeared on the quarter-deck, and, with a ghastly countenance, pointing to his black auxiliary, and scarcely able to speak, he muttered, "It ain't him, sir; it 's his brother." And so it was; for this man had never seen an adze before. Ever afterwards, "as lazy as the Sierra Leone carpenter" was a bye-word; he either could not, or would not do anything.

The colony is divided into five districts, each under the control of a manager, or magistrate, with a salary of 250*l.* a-year. Two of these functionaries were blacks. They decide in nearly all cases, their decisions, however, being subject to an appeal to the governor. They are very often called upon to give judgment in cases requiring equity rather than law, and also in suits of a most delicate nature.

One of these managers, the magistrate of Kent, had to decide in the following cases:—

The custom of the liberated Africans, requires, as a part of the marriage ceremony, that the bridegroom should call on the parents, the day after his marriage, with a present, and openly declare himself satisfied with his bride, and that he had married a virgin.

On the complaint of an old couple, that this custom had not been complied with, the manager sent for the offender, who stated his happiness in the marriage, but pleaded poverty. Being, however, recommended so to do, he borrowed a pound, and ran to his parents-in-law, who received him with open arms, and, in the excess of their exultation, refused the present.

Another custom is, that "man and wife" shall each carry a purse. A husband complained that his wife had been in the habit, during the early days of their connubial state, of making free with both, and on his complaining of this outrageous monopoly, that she had refused him conjugal rights. The manager having remonstrated, desired the husband to report proceedings in a few days—but nothing more was heard upon the subject.

One of the ruling passions of the liberated Africans is, to become a member of some civilized religion, and whence that passion arose must be sought in the proceedings of the members of certain sects. A more blasphemous mode of preaching cannot be imagined. The ridicule of "Peter Simple's" Barbadian Negro preacher, is as nothing, compared with the specimens furnished by the preachers of the Lady Huntingdon and other societies. Series of appeals in the most familiar manner to the Almighty Being are followed, when the lungs of the preacher require rest, by Psalms, adapted to light and popular airs. Some time since the jealousy of the missionaries was aroused by the numerous conversions to Mahommedanism; and for selling charms the Mandingo mosques were closed for a time, to the honour of the colony. They are, however, not interfered with at present, and numbers of converts are annually made, the formerly persecuted religion being favourable to that end, for it is preached entirely by Africans. In nearly every street in Freetown are one or more dissenting chapels.

The liberated African often rises into a man of property, and 8 or 10,000*l.* is by no means an uncommon sum for them to possess. On dashing steeds, they may be seen galloping round the race-course of an evening.

Two in particular, Messrs. Pratt and Isidore, are men of great wealth, and merchants in the colony. To say the truth, there are evil tales told of them ; but large dealings with the former have not altered a good opinion of him.

Mr. Pratt went to England in May—as he himself observed—to educate his elder children, and appoint an agent. Shortly after his arrival, he wrote to express his delight at what he had seen, and at the manner in which he had been treated. He had been taken by a baronet to the House of Lords, of which he was not a little proud. His son told his mother, in a letter, that the pen was an inefficient instrument wherewith to attempt a description, and he greatly regretted that she was not there to witness the wonders of England.

An ex-officer of the colony owed Mr. Pratt some money, and, astonished at seeing him in England, offered him a bill, accepted, as he said, by a nobleman. "Then," replied Mr. Pratt, "if it is the acceptance of so high a personage, you had better cash it and pay me the money." On his next voyage he sent his carpet-bag on board, directed "W. H. Pratt, Esq., cabin-passenger."

This man was a liberated African, and dragged from his country in all the horrors of a slave-ship.

These are two instances, but there are many more. Pratt and Isidore are both Akoos.

The Akoos are the Jews of Africa, and many of them having amassed fortunes, return to their country. They more frequently become converts to Mahommedanism than Christianity; the former offering a plurality of wives, and dealing in charms, and the marvellous accords better with their ideas.

The market is the place to see the inhabitants of Sierra Leone. More languages are spoken there than in any other market in the world; but broken English is the most common. The good humour and ready wit of the negro are remarked at once. It is, however, dangerous to get into conversation with them, for "Beg you for a fipence, massa," is sure to end the palaver, and whether given or not, they always go away laughing.

The liberated Africans come for miles to sell their produce, and almost immediately purchase some article of finery with the money. On a Sunday all are well dressed, and the bright colours give a gaiety to the scene which is very pleasing.

Their villages are generally built on most picturesque spots. Each house cleanly swept round, is encompassed by a garden of fruits and vegetables. Everything about them wears an appearance of happiness and comfort. The roads to the town are crowded during the day, each family sending its portion to the market. In every village there is a Church of England missionary, who superintends the schools. The average number in these schools is 8,000; they are taught reading, writing, and arithmetic.

Sierra Leone exports gold, palm-oil, ivory, ground-nuts, timber, camwood, hides, ginger, pepper, arrowroot, and gum-copal. Of these, the ground-nut trade is the most useful towards the increase of, and demand for labour; and in order to supply the market, the Mandingoes have hired themselves as mercenaries to the Sherbro people, assisting them in their wars for a half-share of the prisoners, whom they make domestic slaves. In September, a boat containing fifty of these was seized, and the slaves emancipated by Mr. Palmer, resident in Kent. The Mandingoes and northern tribes have been known to go as far as the foreign factories at Gallinas to purchase domestic slaves for the carrying on of this trade.

Ground-nuts are generally shipped to France, and manufactured into oil. The liberated Africans cultivate largely; and the soil, with little trouble, will yield large quantities.

The gold is brought from the interior, where many of the natives assert that there are mines; but the general belief is, that it is found in the sands of rivers. It is brought to market in a roughly wrought state, and given in exchange for goods, at an enormous profit to the receiver, as also is ivory.

The palm-oil is extracted simply by treading out or boiling the pulp of the nut, but a superior oil is extracted by boiling the nut itself. Little labour is required, the tree being a native of the forest. The camwood trade might be rendered available for the employment of the African, and increase the demand for labour; while the timber trade, from certain peculiarities attending it, remains in the hands of the Kroomen.

The demand for arrowroot, pepper, ginger, and gum, would employ great numbers of the population of neighbouring States, and render the value of the subject of more avail to the king, and to his owner, than the paltry sum he at present realizes by his being sold.

The increase of the ground-nut trade, and the eager demand for labour consequent upon it, may be fully proved by reference to Colonial Reports from Sierra Leone, and in a measure assist a conviction of the probability that a like demand may be caused for any other production.

The emigrants to Sierra Leone, besides the liberated Africans, are the Kroomen, the free black from Nova Scotia, the Maroon, Mandingo, Foulah, and other northern tribes.

The Kroo, and Fishmen are the most useful of all the African tribes, and seldom fail of getting employment. In their country, although there are considerable numbers of domestic slaves, no foreign slave-trade is allowed. At home, except in canoes, they never work; all labour being performed by slaves.

On the coast, wherever there is trade, there is a Kroo town; and nothing is shipped between Cape Palmas and Sierra Leone, without the assistance of the Kroomen. Although they do not permit the slave-trade in their own country, they ship all the slaves in other countries; the other African tribes being unable to manage the canoes in the surf.

Women never leave the Kroo country, but the emigrants cohabit with liberated African women, and adopt their children.

In Sierra Leone the Krootown is under the superintendance of a headman, who receives a shilling a day, and is held responsible for the good behaviour of his tribe. Besides this he has large emoluments, receiving a fee from all returning and from new members: the superintendant of each street is under him. Every man-of-war and merchant vessel on the coast of Africa ships a number of these auxiliaries; and taking the duty during the rains the white men are preserved from exposure. They enter under the most absurd names, such as "Bottle of Beer," "Flying-jib," "Short-pipe," &c., while others pass as "Prince Albert," "King George," &c. These names are taken for convenience, their own being more difficult to pronounce.

The head Krooman has control over his party, and receives all the pay, slops, and provisions, of which he takes a large share. It is the custom, when a man-of-war is about to return to England, for the Kroomen to purchase all the epaulettes, gold lace, cocked hats, and swords that may not be required; and on a Sunday, Krootown has a most extraordinary appearance. Headed by banners and streamers, and dressed out in all the finery, with drums beating, they parade the town.

Seldom is seen an individual of them with a whole costume: generally one has a coat and epaulettes, a cocked hat, and sword, but no other garment, and sometimes only one article; the wearer being otherwise in a state of nudity.

Besides serving on board ship, they hire themselves out as in-door and out-of-door servants, but they never enlist. The management of the timber trade is almost entirely in their hands, and as many as 2,000 are employed in the Sherbro river alone. They cut it down, and, by means of a light wood called cork-wood, float it to the ship in rafts. This is the most dangerous of our trades with Africa, as, from the weight of the wood, it is necessary to hoist the whole of the raft in as early as possible, and the crew are worked day and night until that is effected; which, added to the vessel being far advanced up a river, generally causes much fever, and not unfrequently death to all. The shipment of the palm-oil, and management of the coasting vessels, are also in the hands of the Kroomen. No Krooman leaves his country but with an idea of returning when his fortune is made: they are generally fine athletic men.

In Africa every tribe has its peculiar mark, by

which, in an assemblage, any man's nation can be at once seen. A notice of some of these may not be uninteresting. The Kroo mark is about half an inch broad, from the forehead over the nose to the chin, and at the outer corner of each eye is a triangular mark.

The Akoo has two lines from the shoulders, meeting in the form of a knot at the lower part of the abdomen.

The Yarriba has three lines from under the arm, round the lower part of the abdomen, and three gashes on either side of the face.

The Jessu's breast is marked like a gridiron: these marks are all cut or burnt in when young, and are indelible.

The Kroomen and Fishmen are reported to be always quarrelling. On board the Bonetta, only one Fishman entered, and nine Kroomen; they were always on good terms.

Their religion is a belief in a good and bad spirit, to which the dead are carried according to their conduct in life. These spirits are ministered to by priests called "Ju-ju," who make sacrifices of bullocks and other animals, portions of which become the property of the priest, while the remainder, excepting the head and blood, which are thrown away, is eaten by the devotees. In these feasts women are forbidden to take part. Their dead are buried without form or ceremony in a convenient hole.

Salt is looked upon in somewhat of a holy light by all Africans. Some members of an interior tribe, assembling at a Palaver at Cape Mount, almost worshipped the sea, and drank so much salt water as to render themselves helpless for several days.

The oath in court is administered to the Krooman by his receiving a small portion of salt, which, having held up towards heaven, he mingles with the dust of the earth; then having tasted it, he considers himself sworn.

The Kroo canoe is simply a hollowed cotton-tree, in which one of the uninitiated would consider himself brave to cross the Serpentine; yet in these frail barks the Kroomen make voyages, and trade between their own country, which is situated on the Grain Coast and Sierra Leone,—a distance of two hundred miles.

The emigrants from Nova Scotia are no great addition to the colony; lazy, and exhibiting a strong taste for dress. They seldom marry, but live in concubinage, and despise the liberated Africans, who, though no blacker than themselves, are designated niggers. It is no less odd than true, that the liberated African in his turn, looks down upon the Krooman, whose position by comparison, is much like that of the Gallego in Portugal, which enables him to make a fortune where the natives would starve. Even on board a ship, the liberated African will not mess with the Krooman, but expects to be placed with the European portion of the crew.

The Maroons are the descendants of the Aborigines of Jamaica, a portion of whom, for creating a civil war, were expatriated. Their love of the colony has been much increased of late years. The emigration to the West Indies having from the traditions of the ancestors of their fatherland, drawn many of them into undertaking the transatlantic voyage, a few were lucky enough to return, which they did with a hearty determination never again to quit the colony. Some of them are industrious, but generally speaking they are, as I have said, lazy and indolent; and the females are exceedingly fond of dress and finery, in which they parade about, a practice which is termed, doing "Yougah,"—showing-off.

The Mandingos, Foulahs, and northern tribes, are all Mahomedans; and besides trading in gold, ivory, and most of the commodities of inland trade, they amass large sums by making converts, who are obliged to assume the garb and purchase the charms. They also hawk about skins, leather-bags, spears, and bridles of their own manufacture. Their costume is very picturesque, consisting of a flowing robe in Summer, of white long-cloth, but in Winter of parti-coloured cloth, a high cap of many colours, leather-sandals, and a number of leather and silver charms about the arms and legs. They are a handsome and tall race.

Mandingo pedlars and priests find their way into the most distant parts of Africa.

The militia are drawn much in the same manner as in England; their dress being rifle. Headed by their band, they form a most respectable body: how they would fight is another question; but no force is requisite to collect them—all being volunteers.

The police, which is regularly embodied, is composed of liberated Africans. One grand complaint is laid against them, which is, that of screening the delinquents who may belong to any of their own tribes. Crime is by no means so common as might be expected, from the extraordinary mixture of the population; except that of murder, which is not unfrequent. A practice prevails called the ordeal of the red water, by which, when able to evade the vigilance of the police, they prove the innocence or otherwise of the party accused. A cup of poison is mixed, and before a "Ju-ju" man, or priest, the condemned one makes oath of his or her innocence As much water is allowed as can be drunk, and should the ordeal not kill, the conviction falls on the accuser, whose life is at the mercy of the accused, and is always taken.

There is one lucrative inland trade, which has not been mentioned,—the fish trade. Eight hundred men are employed in small boats, seven or eight in each. All the fish not sold in the market is half cooked, peppered and salted, and then sent inland. A fisherman often by these means, realizes as much as 30*l*. a month. In this trade all classes of emigrants are employed.

Emigration to the West Indies from the Liberated African Yard is very popular. While

H.M.S. Bonetta lay at Sierra Leone, a large ship arrived for emigrants. She was in every way well found; and besides a surgeon, to attend not only to the health of the emigrants, but also to report on their diet, &c., she had as agent for herself and another vessel, a commander in her majesty's navy—as an inducement to the negro. She had a brass band on board, which was, by no means, a slight attraction. What a contrast must be observable between these vessels and the slave-ship, by those who have such ample opportunities of judging!

The emigration is carried on under an agent, who receives a salary of 250*l.* per annum, and a guinea a head for each emigrant. A French steamer-of-war being at Sierra Leone, her commander was ordered to examine and report on the system, with a view to follow it up if it were found to answer. He described to a British officer that he could not but praise it highly; but as for recommending it, the plan was too expensive for his Government.

It has been the object of this chapter to point out Sierra Leone, in its relation to the slave-trade; it must not be considered, therefore, as a description of that colony, nor must the manners, &c., of the liberated Africans be looked upon as particularly descriptive of their various nations, but perhaps of what they would be, had they the same opportunities opened to them, by means of a fair and honest trade. As a proof of this, the Akoos or Yarribas are said to be of the very worst class of idolators, and certainly the greatest traffickers in slaves of the whole coast. Yet they succeed better than any other ; while those whose countries are situated within sight of Sierra Leone, and who are shipped from the Gallinas, are generally the most indolent and worst of the emigrants, though at home there is less idolatry or evil exercised ; the cause of their embarkation being merely a war, excited by the slave-merchants for their own purposes.

CHAPTER III.

CAPE MOUNT.

As this country from its internal broils underwent an entire change during the period H.M.S. Bonetta was on the northern division, a description of these revolutions and their consequent effects on the slave-trade, together with some account of the state of society, and manners and customs of the people, may be interesting to the general reader.

Africans, although they have no works wherein to record the deeds of their ancestors, nor any knowledge of the formation of a genealogical tree, can and do, notwithstanding, open a debate or a "palaver" with an inquiry into ancestry for periods of two and three hundred years, bringing it down correctly to the present day, and claiming without mistake cousinship as distant as that known in Scotland. Hereditary families hold thrones for centuries, and although primogeniture is by no means a condition, and even at times usurpers seize and retain the throne, yet when the descendant of the old stock is looked for by his countrymen, whatever the lapse of years may be, he is generally found. Should a country fall into a state of anarchy, either by the aggression of a hostile state or the rebellion of its subjects, should a powerful warrior or a scheming demagogue seize the reins of power, the neighbouring chiefs shew him no respect farther than that exacted by fear, and his person is at all times exposed to the jealousy or hatred of his neighbours, who, in order to get rid of him, are by no means slow at poison or other secret modes of murder.

The actual power of a chief or king has been much exaggerated; it may be condensed in one word—custom—which is paramount in Africa. Innovations are looked upon with suspicion, and generally the promoter of them at least falls a victim. Old customs must be kept up, however much they may be disliked by the chief. The king is married into every family of note in his kingdom, and cannot perform any national act without collecting the whole of the heads of these to "palaver;" and should he neglect to do so, or alter any established rule of the country, he is almost certain to perish for his temerity.

In many respects the rule of African States is patriarchal; all complaints, however trifling, are made to the king, or, if he be at a distance, to the head man of the district, whose decision is subject to an appeal to the sovereign, as an instance to be mentioned presently will shew. The extreme punishment for minor crimes is the yielding up by the culprit of his liberty to the offended party, the former becoming a domestic slave either for life or for some definite period, or he has to supply one or more substitutes, according to the crime. Thus, for instance, a Siberian citizen, resident at Cape Mount, had his house entered by thieves, and complaining of it, the king set the ju-ju men (priests) to find the burglars, who, exciting their fears, soon brought about a confession. They were sentenced to supply to the injured party three domestic slaves of tender age, to be his property until they attained their twentieth year.

The people of Cape Mount are generally considered more enlightened than their coast neighbours. Their language is of the purest of the

African dialects, and is spoken far inland. It is called the Vohie language, taking its name from an interior country. Until 1840 the slave-trade was carried on here with great success, the bay offering one of the best anchorages, and the beach being freer from surf than in any part of the northern coast; and during the earlier periods it was a most extensive resort of slavers.

Gradually, from the effect of treaties and presents, the trade was entirely stopped, and but for the indefatigable and extraordinary proceedings of one, would perhaps have remained so. In order thoroughly to explain this, it will be necessary to lay before the reader the few treaties that have been made, and their effects.

Cape Mount was governed in 1841 by a king named Fano-toro, who unfortunately fell into the snares of a slave-merchant, a Florentine by birth, but English, French, or American when convenience suited, who dexterously managed to humbug the sovereign into transferring his kingdom (under the protection of the British flag) to himself. At least so runs the document.

COPY OF THE GRANT.

"Know all men by these presents that I, Fano-toro, king of Grand Cape Mount and its dependencies, in the presence and with full consent of my principal chiefs assembled, in consideration of a mutual friendship existing between Theodore Canot and Co., British subjects, and myself, the particulars whereof are under written, do for myself and heirs and successors give and grant unto the said, &c., their heirs and assignees in perpetuity, all the land under the name of Cape Mount (here follows a description of the State), subject to the authority and dominion of H.M. the Queen of Great Britain, her heirs and successors. (Here right of trade, &c.)

"Dated under the royal hand and seal, at the town of Fana-nea.

"FANO-TORO, *King*.
"GREY, *Prince*."

Febuary 23, 1841.

This document purports to be witnessed by Lieutenant Seagrave, of her Majesty's service, and a P.S. states that the Hon. Captain Denman visited and reported most favourably of the colony.

Lieutenant Seagrave could hardly have been a

witness to the above, for it appears that on the 21st February, 1841, he effected a treaty with King Fano-toro, wherein it was stated that on his part, the king should, as far as lay in his power, put a stop to the slave-trade; on the part of Lieutenant Seagrave, that H. M. Government should make a yearly present so long as the treaty was strictly kept.

This treaty must have been "a heavy blow and a great discouragement" to the interests of Canot, who was a slave-dealer on a large scale, and resident as well in Cape Mount, as in the Solyman river (Gallinas). In order to frustrate the object of the treaty, Canot must have framed the grant; however that may be, the territory was advertised in the "Times," and a highly respectable Prussian merchant in Sierra Leone, stated that H.M. of Prussia had been so intent on the purchase, as to have written to him on the subject of the validity of Canot's claims, which were, of course, annulled.

In order definitively and for ever to get rid of the obnoxious treaty, Canot, on July 18th, 1844, thus addresses himself to Sir W. Daniell, Com. R.N., then senior officer at Sierra Leone.

"I have made King Fano-toro acquainted with the approval of H.M. Government of the agreement signed 21st February, 1841, with its additional articles (the main object of which is the abolition of the slave-trade).

"The king begs to inform you that the above-mentioned agreement was signed and stipulated in conjunction with others whom H.M. Government pleases not to sanction* and that the fair-spoken promises of Captain Tucker, R.N., of a yearly present, not having been attended to since the signing of the above-mentioned document, and that he, Fano-Toro, having on his part, strictly kept his promise not to allow the shipment of slaves out of his territory, cannot consider himself bound to adhere to either of them, therefore he will consider all those agreements entered into between himself and Lieutenant Seagrave, Captains Tucker and Denman, R.N. as null and void.

Signed, "CANOT."

This is dated from "New Florence," Canot's name for the territory of Cape Mount.

How far the king himself was connected with

* The pretended cession is here of course implied.

the above, or the cession of his dominions, the following letter from Commodore Jones may illustrate.

From Commodore Jones, R.N., to King Fano-toro.

"In compliance with your request, I send you a copy of the printed instrument in my possession, which purports to be a full cession of your country, made by you and your chiefs, to Mr. Theodore Canot and his partner, Mr. Redman, a British subject.

"The British officer, Lieutenant Seagrave, who is said to have witnessed that agreement, exceeded his authority if he did so.

"But the British Government—seeing the unjust and, on your part, the improvident nature of the transaction, and that it was even attempted to implicate its own name as a guarantee of the agreement and protector of Cape Mount, which was thus ceded, in full property, to Messrs. Redman and Canot — refused its sanction, as you are aware. Formal notice was given to you from the British squadron of such refusal. This paternal measure, on the part of the British Government, should have been received by you as a new proof of the anxious desire of the Queen's Government to be just to the natives of this coast, and not upon any pretext to usurp or encroach on their natural rights, either openly or indirectly.

"But, instead of this, and your receiving the Queen's goodness in a right spirit, we are told, in your name, that you consider all engagements between us at an end and virtually dissolved. And accordingly, it soon became known that the slave-trade was revived in your country, and that persons residing within your jurisdiction were active agents in carrying it on.

"To these great offences, in breach of the engagements which still subsisted between us in full force, and which you had no power to put an end to without our consent, I was preparing to apply a remedy, which would, doubtless, have proved effectual. But the proper manner in which you have met my representations, and on this day have renewed and confirmed the existing treaties, has happily spared me from the pain of having recourse to any unfriendly act of superior power. I heartily rejoice at this wiser and better termination of our differences, and I earnestly recommend you, O King, and the Chiefs of Cape Mount, to disregard the counsel of evil* advisers, and to merit, by your faithful performance of the treaties in future, that protection from the Government of my gracious Mistress the Queen, which will not be withheld from those who prove themselves not unworthy of Her favour and bounty.

"I wish you, King Fan-toro, and your chiefs and people, health and prosperity, and am, &c.,

"W. JONES."

In order to dismiss this part of our subject, it is necessary, perhaps, to add that shortly after, at the demand of Captain Murray, R.N., that the treaty should be maintained, the treaty of Canot, at Cape Mount, was burnt by the order of the King, the English being witnesses, and Canot was taken prisoner to America, he being then a *soi disant* American, and sailing a slave-barque under the American flag. It has lately been reported that he gained his cause in America and damages for demurrage.

On the 2nd of January, 1846, the following final treaty was entered into, and it is with a view of

* Fano-toro's successor, as will presently be seen, was murdered for supporting this treaty, and at the instigation of this very evil adviser,—Canot.

illustrating its effects on the people, that the following chapters have been written.

Engagement between Her Majesty the Queen of England and the chiefs of Cape Mount, for the suppression of the slave-trade.

At an adjourned meeting and solemn palaver, held on the banks of the river Cape Mount, within, at the bar, this 2nd of January, 1846, between King Fano-toro, the Chief of Cape Mount, his chiefs and head men, and other chiefs of the neighbourhood, on the one part, and Commander J. W. D. Brisbane, commander of H.M.S. the Larne, on the part of Her Majesty the Queen of England. The said chiefs, on the part of themselves, their heirs, and successors, have agreed upon the following articles and conditions:—

Article I.

The engagement between King Fano-toro, Prince Grey, and the head men of Cape Mount, and Lieut. Seagrave, of the British Navy, on the 21st of February, 1841, is hereby fully admitted to be binding on the said King Fano-toro, his chiefs, and head men, their heirs, and successors.

All the provisions of that engagement, for the suppression of the slave-trade, remain, and are to continue in force, and are hereby confirmed, and the export of slaves to foreign countries is for ever abolished, in the territories of the chiefs of Cape Mount: and the chiefs of Cape Mount engage to make and proclaim a law, prohibiting any of their subjects, or any person within their jurisdiction, from selling, or assisting in the sale of any slave for transportation to a foreign country: and the chiefs of Cape Mount promise to inflict a severe punishment on any person who shall break this law.

II.

No European, or other person whatever, shall be permitted to reside within the territories of the chiefs of Cape Mount, for the purpose of carrying on, in any way, the traffic in slaves, and no houses, or stores, or buildings, of any kind whatever, shall be erected for the purpose of slave-trade, within the territory of the chiefs of Cape Mount.

If at any time it shall appear that slave-trade has been carried on through, or from the territory of the chiefs of Cape Mount, the slave-trade may be put down by Great Britain, by force upon that country, and British officers may seize the boats or vessels of Cape Mount, found anywhere carrying on the slave-trade; and the chiefs of Cape Mount will subject themselves to a severe act of displeasure on the part of the Queen of England.

IV.

The subjects of the Queen of England may always trade freely with the people of Cape Mount, in every article they may wish to buy and sell, in all the places, ports, and rivers, within the territories of the chiefs of Cape Mount, and throughout the whole of their dominions, and the chiefs of Cape Mount pledge themselves to shew no favour, and give no privilege to the ships and trades of other countries, which they do not shew to those of England.

Given under our hands and seals, in the river of Cape Mount, this 2nd day of January, 1846.

his
KING X FANO-TORO,
GEORGE X CAIN, Chief,
TOM X LEVEN, Chief.

(Signed) JOHN WILLIAM DOUGLAS BRISBANE,
Commanding H.B.M.S. Larne.

By virtue of the power deputed to me, I hereby declare the approval of the Queen, my mistress, to the above engagement.

Given under my hand, on board H.M.S. Penelope, this 2nd January, 1846.

(Signed) W. Jones,
Commodore and senior officer, commanding
British squadron.

The foregoing treaty was signed, sealed, and delivered, in our presence—

R. D. Powel, Lieutenant, Penelope,
Thomas Etheredge, ditto, Larne,
E. A. Schomberg, ditto, H.M.S. Penelope,
John Hay, acting P. and P. Larne,
Theodore Canot, settler, Cape Mount.

The above treaty, the destruction of the factories of Mr. Canot, together with a promise of a yearly present, might be said to have finally stopped the slave-trade at Cape Mount.

Internal wars commenced, and, in consequence of this determined attack on the laws and customs, Fano-toro, in his old age, afraid to leave his country to a half-witted son, pitched upon a famous warrior, whom he nominated his successor, and abdicated; leaving Prince George Cain to be governor of a kingdom, at war with all its neighbours far and wide.

This new king not only ruled, hated by his neighbours as being an upstart, but also as being the supporter of one of those infringements of custom; an infringement so little relished by the African chiefs, whose territories lying inland, had all to lose and nothing to gain by the adhesion of Cape Mount to the anti-slave-trade treaty.

Having conquered all his former enemies, and, in some instances, made them his subjects, he sent this defiance to a distant monarch: "Like an old goat your beard must be long from inactivity; come and make a war with me, and I will shear it." These words were told at a conference after his death, by the chief to whom they were addressed. King Cain imagined himself secure: a few short months told a far different tale, and proved the almost total impossibility of putting a stop to the slave-trade, without thoroughly introducing an equivalent, or, at all events, some trade as a substitute.

Although great promises of trading were held

out, it can only be presumed it was found impossible for the British government to obtain any; as from the year 1841, when the slave-trade was supposed to have been first put a stop to, until 1848, when it might be said to have recommenced, the country of Cape Mount, holding the finest anchorage on that part of the coast, never received in its bay one single British or other merchant vessel; and a most lucrative trade had been relinquished by the chief against the will of the people, for what? for a present that he himself pocketed!

And what were the consequences? Read the next chapters, and they will unfold.

CHAPTER IV.

CAPE MOUNT.

It is necessary, for the sake of distinction, to speak of kings, courts, and regal state. An excellent history of one of these monarchs may be found in the once popular ballad, the "King of the Cannibal Islands;" wherein the description of palace and harem are truly depicted. In order to prepare the reader, and as a slight sketch of the private life of my friend, before entering on his public character, it may not be out of place to give the following anecdotes.

H.M.S. Amphitrite visited Cape Mount, and King Cain visited the Amphitrite. Received by salute and guard, he retired into the captain's cabin, where, throwing off the monarch, he condescended to converse on various matters. The whim of the moment led an officer, who sat next to him, to bargain for the royal robes; and, after a short discussion, the king received a quantity of pretty glazed printed calico. The Mandingo dress was to be retained until the salute was over, and honours had been paid on his departure. Relying on the royal word, the officer left the captain's cabin, and descended to his mess to dinner, which he had scarcely commenced when the guns fired, and, reaching the deck, he found king and calico both gone, and neither did he see again.

When we paid him a visit, on leaving his interior town, a bottle of wine had been stowed away, deep in the recesses of a market basket. The king anxiously inquired if any more could be spared, and was told that only one bottle remained, and that that was reserved. A halt before wishing him good-bye occurred. When, in the heat of the day, we sought our bottle, it was gone: the king had abstracted it!

Three of his wives accompanying us in an excursion, the doctor observing the arm of one of these ladies to be decorated with an English half-crown, had two others slung, and presenting them to the king, asked him to deliver them to the other two. He expressed his willingness, provided a third was given, as the other might be jealous. A short time afterwards, having some monetary transactions on shore, one of these half-crowns was given as change.

King Cain, so called by English visitors, was a man about eight-and-twenty, tall, well-built, and for a black handsome. At his birth he had been called Zĕnāh. Becoming a member of the secret society called the Pourra (of which in its place) he took the name of Bahi, by a contraction of Bahi-zenah, which might be called his country name. On his conversion he took the Mahomedan name of Bryhemah (Abraham) and being a warrior went to battle as Tumbeh.

He was a clever man, and had he lived his family might have been the means of spreading civilization over that part of Africa. Already he had four sons at Christian, and two at Mahomedan schools. His life had been passed as a warrior, and being brave, he was generous, and although surrounded by enemies, he was seldom the aggressor.

Cape Mount is situated between Gallinas, and the free country of Liberia. From its position, and the facility it offers to the trader, every endeavour should be made to suppress the slave-trade, by encouraging industry in manufactures, agriculture, &c., or in other words by establishing a lucrative and legitimate trade.

Having received the king with a salute, and a present, he, in return, gave a supper. Shortly after landing, the revels commenced by the performance of several war-dances to the sound of the tom-toms or drums, the king's wives singing and exciting the warriors. The palace was a round mud house, white-washed inside and out, consisting of one large room, in which was some English furniture that had been presented by different foreign friends. Having retired from the dances, a huge black ram, carried by two sturdy blacks, each holding two legs, was introduced and danced about for at least a quarter of an hour, after which, immediately outside the door, it was slaughtered, and in less than an hour re-appeared, cooked in a dozen different ways, the most novel and best of which was the Palaver sauce, a favourite African dish, made of greens, palm-oil, fish, meat, &c., chopped small, and spread out on boiled rice. No females were allowed at this banquet, except as attendants.* Having brought

* Once giving a dinner, on board, to the King of Mumna,

some liquors from the ship, we made an excellent supper, and going on board, made arrangements for an excursion to a farm residence of the king's next day.

The Beach town of Cape Mount stands on a neck of sand to the north-east of the Cape, which forms a bar to the river. It is small, but of much importance, being the principal salt-manufactory in the kingdom; which, as in most countries, is a royal monopoly, and here is one of the currencies of the country. Having launched the boat over this neck of sand, at five in the morning, we started off "Turrah-Gourral" (or under the shade of the Turroh tree). The party consisted of the king and some of his *attachés*, bearing a spare dress, an umbrella, a single-barrelled fowling-piece, &c., Dr. Campbell, and myself and the rowers, and six Kroomen. Numerous small green islands being passed, we opened on the lake Pishermanee, and at nine o'clock reached the town of Bŭdah (the state). A fine-looking old man came out to receive us: Mousa (or Moses), the head-man. Bŭdah is

we having desired his attendants to sit down, he indignantly asked if it was thought he could eat with his servants. Placing two salt-cellars between ourselves and the followers, he was satisfied when told it was a royal custom in Scotland.

a stockaded town; the piles are driven very closely together, and lashed with bamboos, standing about twelve feet from the ground, of which there was a double row. In formation, it was nearly a circle, and entered by two gates, cut solid out of the huge cotton tree. The town was clean, the houses low and open, built of mud, and with no furniture in them. In the centre lay four large logs at right angles, the ends meeting; these formed the fire, and were separated or closed according to the heat required: in various parts were hung hammocks, made of a strong grass and mats. About the town, and in the houses, roamed bullocks, sheep, goats, fowls, and ducks. From a square, the houses were irregularly built (a passage between them), so that each had a street round. Outside the town were large clearances, in which grew rice, ground-nuts, pumpkins, and cassado. At a short distance were the remains of a stockaded town, and near them a perfect golgotha. On inquiring the cause of these bleaching bones, the king related the following:

"Some time ago one Nuyaqui-Tumbǧh, a warrior, made war here, and being defeated, himself and the greater part of his warriors were slain.

Moussa, afraid of another attack, razed the town, and built the new Bŭdah."

This we afterwards found was not the case, and a savage glance from Moussa told it could not be. It appears that Bŭdah (the state) was so called because, in earlier days, it was an independent state, in the heart of Cape Mount territory. Cain, as a war-man of Fano-toro's, had destroyed it; but, on becoming king, he had allowed the hereditary chief Moussa to build a new town, and had placed him in it as head-man, and Moussa, though apparently a friend, was a bitter enemy. Having breakfasted, and allowed Moussa to join us, we proceeded to Turroh-Gourral, situated on a hill, about four miles up a creek branching from the Pishermanie, a most picturesque town, well supplied with cattle and grain. This was entirely the property of the king, and filled with his family, who regaled us with a capital dinner of fish, flesh, and fowl.

On our return the party was increased by three of the royal wives, who beguiled the time by relieving the boat's crew in singing. Their songs were extempore, and spoke of the serenity of the evening, the strangeness of their situation, in honour of their lord and master and his foreign friends, &c. By nine we were on board the ship having passed a most pleasant day.

In order to give an account of a trip to the capital, distant about forty miles in the interior, it is necessary to introduce another African King, called by the English, Robin, King of Manna; at his birth he was named Far, which, annexed to his Pourro name, became Pa-Far. His Mahomedan name was Marmoroo, and the war-titles of Hagua and Coêh, two of the Eagle tribe, were by no means misplaced. An African Dugald Dalgetty, ready to fight for any one, and a renowned warrior, he had been wounded in the hip: he had a shortened right leg, and had received a bullet through the groin and two through the right shoulder, besides the loss of two fingers of the right hand. He had not an idea beyond fighting and drinking, for both of which he was justly famed. He never moved out without two bards, who continually sang his praises in the most lusty manner. Visiting the Bonetta, he brought his secretary (*soi disant*), who had been educated at Sierra Leone. Having expressed a wish to see his handwriting, he sat down and wrote as follows:—

"Sir,—I am happy to have the opportunity of addressing you, and hope you will make me a little present. (Signed) "PANDOO."

The ready and native wit did not go unrewarded.

Cain was at his capital, so having promised him a visit there, taking advantage of a cessation of the rains, with Robin as guide, we set out, having three days' provisions, and some liquor, as a present, in our canteen. At Turrah-Gourral we breakfasted, and were surprised at finding all the inhabitants absent, being, we were told, at the capital on a palaver. On leaving this town, the creek was so narrow, paddles were substituted for oars. The scenery was most beautiful: overhead, the trees joined and perfectly hid the sky; the vegetation was extremely luxuriant and bedecked with most beautiful flowers; birds of magnificent plumage flew about in all directions, and gave to the scene a fairy effect. Fifteen miles brought us to a landing, when, diving into the mysteries of a virgin forest, at a distance of about six miles, we emerged on a clearance, in the centre of which, surrounded by a pleasant *bosquet*, and situate on the banks of a purling stream, stood a picturesque village. Large rice and ground-nut fields lay on all sides, and a pleasant greeting was given by the inhabitants, many of whom for the first time gazed on white men.

Leaving this farm, another forest-path opened on a similar one, while a third opened on a stockaded town, called Manina (half town). The path hitherto had been a mere track, but now opened on a broad road in good condition. Passing through a pleasant *bosquet*, we came abruptly on the banks of a large river, across which was a floating-bridge. On the opposite side stood the capital Gononamarro (new stockade).

The king, having been warned of our vicinity, stood on the opposite banks to receive us, backed by almost all the inhabitants, while at our rear followed hundreds from Manina. The bright colours in the light dresses of the natives beautifully adorned the banks (while the river itself was a perfect field of lilies), and the huge stockaded town behind, presented a most novel and striking scene.

Robin marshalled us across, but it did not require a second glance at the king, to detect that his jealousy was roused by the presence of the neighbour chief, nor was his naturally-good temper revived during the visit. The town was certainly very large, and strongly stockaded. Between each row of piles (a distance of eight feet) was a pack of bamboo pikes; there were several squares, one of which was occupied by the various houses forming the king's palace. There were no regular streets, but innumerable passages. The best house in the town was the Mahomedan mosque, nicely white-washed inside and out, and laid with mats. The Mandingo priest invited us to an inspection of his dwelling, which was very clean. He had a number of religious works, many of them manuscripts, and one was a copy of the Koran, in Arabic, printed in London. The school is held at dusk: a large fire is lighted in front of the mosque, and round it sit the scholars, each supplied with boards and books. They read aloud, and, apparently, understand but little; the evening's lesson closes with a prayer, in which all join.

In the middle of the large square is the Gre-gre, a post, surrounded by rough stones: under this are placed sundry charms, for the protection of the town, and on the stones the warriors sharpen their weapons, and thus acquire increased confidence in them. In these squares are rough tombstones to the more wealthy deceased inhabitants.

The king had a quantity of gin, purchased from Liberia. Robin, not content with what we gave him, was anxious to purchase some; the king's ill-humour would not allow him to give any, and he made us become security for the payment, at which Robin was very indignant.

In the evening the head-man of Turroh-Gourral begged our intercession with the king, his subjects having appealed against him. By pleading the novelty of the white man's visit, the business was settled, and the head-man allowed to sit in our assembly.

On the following day we returned. On leaving Gononamarro, the Mahomedan priest made his appearance, out of breath, to tell us he wished to make a present. We protested, but he insisted; saying, as a bookman he ought, as we were bookmen: against this we could not argue. "It will be here directly," he remarked; adding, he had sent to Manina for some fowls for us. As we were going towards Manina, not liking to take the good priest out of his way, we begged he would receive a present in return, and we gave him a few silver pieces. "You can take them when you meet them," he said; but we saw neither priest nor present after.

The above excursions are only two out of many we made.

The inhabitants are peaceable and well disposed, as compared with their neighbours. The costume varies according to the means of the wearer. The most common is a loose piece of country-made cloth thrown over the shoulders, and reaching to the feet. Not a little foppery is shewn in the mode of dressing the woolly hair, which is plaited into all sorts of shapes.

The diet is very simple: meat is seldom used; fowls and ducks only by the wealthy, while the general food is either rice, foo-foo, or palaver sauce. Foo-foo is a kind of paste made of pounded cassado, which is so tenacious that it is swallowed at once. Fish is seldom caught by the natives, but bought at times from the Kroomen. They have few luxuries, and in a household all fare alike, master and slave.

The money of the country is, the bar (Néahcoluh), made of steel, in shape like an elongated miniature spade, about fourteen inches long, about one shilling of our money, equivalent to which are—

The bar of salt,—salt in a parcel three feet high, and three inches in diameter.

The cloth bar, a piece of country cloth uncoloured.

Five heads of tobacco.

A fathom of long cloth.

A bottle of rum.

Two handfuls of gunpowder.

One musket is about ten bars.

One domestic slave, sixty bars.

But any silver money is taken, and is made into ornaments. Bullocks and wives are considered as the signs of wealth.

The agriculture of this part of Africa is a matter by no means difficult: the soil is rich in the extreme, and requires but little cultivation. The man clears the ground and hoes it, then sits down; the woman sows, weeds, and scares the birds away. When the harvest time comes, the man reaps, thrashes, and stores, and the woman makes the grain available. The weeds grow so fast during the rainy season, that, being cut down, they are dried by the scorching sun, and hoed into a manure. Irrigation is not requisite, and rice will grow on uplands moistened by the tremendous rains. The only implement is the hoe.

The manufactures are salt, country cloth, and ground-nut and palm-oils.

Salt is procured by simply boiling the salt-water in their brass pans, and taking therefrom the crystallized particles.

Country cloth:—the cotton grows wild, and, being spun, is dyed; it is then woven on a loom, about six inches wide; any number of these widths which may be required are sewed together.

The colours of the dyes are red, blue, yellow, and green. Camwood makes the red; the blue is from the leaf of a green bush, called the Serang; the leaf, dried and pulverized, is sized, a glue made of the thorns of the cotton tree; yellow is the sap of a tree called Bassel; and green, the two mixed. These dyes, except the green, keep their colour well, and are very brilliant.

The forests abound in game of all kinds, deer of several species, wild hog, &c., besides leopards, elephants, and boa constrictors.

The gutta percha is among the giants of the

forest, as also African oak, cotton, mahogany, and several other useful and handsome woods.

Palm wine and palm cabbage trees grow in all parts, and are both excellent in their way.

The people are indolent, and as long as they have a sufficient present quantity of cassado, rice, or ground-nuts, would consider it far too much trouble to work for more.

In Cape Mount they differ from most parts of Africa, for all religions are tolerated, The ancient religion is termed Gre-Gre, of which there are priests. What the tenets of the religion are, no one could explain; one of the points of faith is, that after death the spirit re-appears over the place of burial, and unless fed in the usual manner while on earth, will become troublesome. The Alligator is one of the deities, and is considered a friend to man. The devotees place living sacrifices of sheep, fowls, &c., in the vicinity of their haunts, and having delivered an oration, quit the spot. After some time, they return and open another palaver. Another mode of sacrifice is the following:—should one be on his death-bed, he vows if he recovers to set at liberty a fowl, bullock, or sometimes, a slave.

Human sacrifices seldom occur, although frequent in countries south; the only instances are on the eve of a war. The ju-ju (priest) recommends one or more slaves being impaled to ensure success.

The king is a Mahomedan, as also all the chiefs, and in short nearly all the people.

The king is law-giver, and in himself alone has the power of life and death. Theft is more regarded as a crime than murder, which is seldom brought to light.

For various offences criminals are staked to the ground for days, weeks, and months, or whipped with a leather thong.

There is a secret society in Cape Mount, as in most countries, called the Pourra Society. The rules are mutual assistance, sworn secrecy, to such an extent, that if one should reveal anything in a distant country, his brethren will travel after him, determined to kill him wherever they may meet him. Of course, they have many other rules, which, from the above reason, are kept pretty secret. The application of the gridiron is really in use among the Pourra men, and the initiated are marked by a hot iron, from the lower end of the back-bone to the shoulder-blades.

In the vicinity of every town is a Pourra bush, and, during a meeting, it is certain death to be found in it. The term used by the natives is, "burying wisdom." The elder brethren, dressed as demons and wild men, with fearful howls and imprecations, raise, as they pretend, the devil, and by his art name the candidate. A feast ensues, after considerable noise and howling, and shriekings, perfectly bewildering, and exciting the curiosity of the uninitiated.

At a conference held at the Beach-town, a very respectable native band played all the time. It consisted of ten performers, eight of whom played upon elephants' trunks, of various sizes, some being very large: the large end was covered with leopard's skin, while near the small end was a mouth-piece. The other instruments were country drums.

Africans are great gamblers, and there are several games of chance at Cape Mount. One of these, called Po, is a warlike game. Each has a side of a board, pierced with twelve round holes; in each hole are four men. They commence by what is called making a town, which is, by each collecting all his men into one hole; they then sally, and if a man can pass right round, putting one in each hole until he reach his own town, he huffs all those he has passed over, and so on, till the board is clear. At times, they become so excited at this game, as to sell even the cloth of decency they wear.

The weapons are spears and swords, but of late years the introduction of muskets and guns, in no small quantity, has taken place. In a town, a guard is set, night and day, armed, and the watches of the night are called; while in the bush, and on the frontiers, a constant picquet is kept.

The moment the child is born, the mother, with the infant in her arms, starts for the nearest water (the sea is preferred), and bathes. Nine-tenths of the population are born slaves, that is to say, the property of the remaining tenth; and thus the child, although born free, is almost sure of becoming the property of the mother's owners, either by sale, or from the affection she bears the father. Domestic slaves are not sold, unless some charge can be proved against them, and it is at all times easy to manage that; but the children thus sold, are looked upon as *bonâ fide* slaves, and it is in this manner that the markets are partly supplied, and thus, those hellish, floating miseries, too often met with, may be accounted for. The birth of a child is a source of no pleasure to father or mother: no natural ties, in any grade of society, seem to be acknowledged. If the father be a head-man, he has a plurality of wives, and if a king, hundreds; and the female offspring are given, at a most tender age, to other head-men and sovereigns, as presents of conciliation and friendship. A poor man, on the other hand, would not be able to bring up a daughter, and consequently sells her. Boys have a better fate, as, be there ever so many, the head-man and the king are proud of them, and the poor man is often able to get his children adopted by his more wealthy neighbour.

Marriage is an affair only common among the richer classes; King Cain had one hundred and seventy wives, the greater part of them under twelve years of age; while the matron of the harem and chief wife was not more than his own age. By these wives he had thirty children. A head-man of a town or district, will have as many as twenty and thirty wives, one of which will be either a sister or daughter of the king's; by which, having given the king a relation, a sort of family connection arises that makes the king simply the head of one large family; for below these all are slaves to the king and head-man, and their offspring.

Wives are looked upon much in the same light as a farmer in England looks upon his cattle. They work upon his farm, and perform all household and out-of-door offices. A man's wealth is judged in two ways,—by the number of bullocks he keeps and the number of his wives. Strange as it may appear, the bullocks roam about, eat, drink, and sleep; and, except for sacrifices and grand feasts, are never killed or parted with except to add one to the harem; when, unless the acquisition be a beauty, a fat kine is considered equivalent. In these harems there is much intrigue, which is generally punished with death to the offenders. Robin once quaintly remarked, pointing to a handsome black, "That 's my brother, and yet he 's not my brother. His mother was my father's wife, but another man loved her, and that is the consequence."

The poor man has but few chances of contracting a marriage, unless he turn war-man; when, by making himself in the least conspicuous, he has a prisoner given to him to wife.

There is no ceremony on either side, except in cases of barter, unless—and it seldom happens—a negro Cupid should have visited the couple, and then a present must be given to the parents of the girl.

Death, according to the followers of the Gre-Gre, or worshippers of the Alligator, is a removal to a better state, and little cared for. When a king dies, all the subjects mourn by shaving a portion or all of their heads, and wearing a grass rope round their necks. Women howl for hours every sun-set and sunrise for six weeks. The remains are bound in country cloth, so many and tight that no effluvia can escape; a hole is dug in the ground, and in it a pile is erected, on which the mummy is placed, and then thatched over. In this way a current of air is constantly passing, and thus the body is left until the necessaries for a wake are arranged, liquor being the staple commodity for that purpose. This sometimes takes months in collecting. Amidst feasting, drinking, and rioting, the remains of the parent and husband are closed over by his half hundred progeny and hundreds of wives, all drunk or as nearly so as they can afford to be. Head-men are buried much in the same manner, but wailed over only by a proportionate number. Thus, while we were at Cape Mount, three of the royal harem died: the first was the daughter of a neighbouring king, and was bewailed by all the living ones; the last was the daughter of a petty chief, and one of her late companions only bewailed her.

The poor man is put into a hole and covered over; but the spirits of all are fed after death, for a short time at least; Guanas, Ants, Lizards, &c., devouring the whole of the food before morning. In cases of war, enemies are never buried.

One day Robin asked, indignantly, how he could be thought guilty of burying a dead enemy. He threw them into the bush and the cattle ate them. Should a man feel unwell he lies down to die, and is only astonished when he gets up again.

CHAPTER V.

CAPE MOUNT.

Treaties had been arranged which, added to purchases made by the Liberian government, were said to have entirely put down the slave-trade, excepting only at Gallinas, on the line of coast from Sierra Leone to Cape Palmas. It is to shew of how little avail these treaties were, and the awful responsibility incurred by the kings, that the present chapter is written.

King Fortune, of Kittam, sent his brother to Sierra Leone, to obtain a promise of trading, in which he failed; — the Kittam shores are inhospitable. King Fortune sent the same brother to Gallinas, and bargained for a payment of four, five, and six hundred bars for each shipment, according to numbers.

King Fortune was an African prince of very ancient family, and, for his country, a rich man. Unfortunately for him, the Gallinas merchants had an evil eye towards his territory, and, in common with the rest of their neighbours, he received the threat, "Open your shores to our trade, or we will make war with you." The threat, however, was accompanied by a promise of remuneration in the event of his acquiescence.

Having signed the anti-slave-trade treaty, the king, although beset by his subjects, made an attempt to open a trade, and to one merchant in Sierra Leone he offered an exchange in barter of 200*l.* worth of camwood, as a commencement.

Finding no trade forthcoming, he had no alternative but at once to close with the Gallinas people; as his own subjects, divested of the power of gain in any way, would, most probably, get rid of him had he not done so.

When he signed the treaty, he did so with the understanding on both sides, that the Gallinas merchants were too strong for him to make war with, but that he would do all in his power, and if any slaving was going on in his territory, he would hoist a white flag to the cruizer. While his brother was at Sierra Leone he faithfully did so, but as soon as he leagued with the Gallinas people he gave it up.

The slave-merchants declared open war against Robin, of Manna, and promised to continue it until Manna was opened to their trade. It has been remarked elsewhere, that Robin's forte was war, and he madly pursued it, constantly appealing to his British allies for assistance, but in vain. His prisoners of war were sold, not, "as he indignantly refuted," to the Spaniards, but to his neighbours, for bullocks, and his neighbours made a most lucrative trade in re-selling them to the Spaniards, who, notwithstanding they had been their mercenaries, received them now as merchandize, and shipped them across the seas.

Robin was also one of a long line of ancestors, and although he abided by the treaty made with him, still, unwittingly, as has been shewn, he most seriously assisted the foreign trade. One hundred and forty of his private slaves and wives were taken prisoners alone, and the captures he made (nearly all of whom reverted to the Spaniards) filled the barracoons.

Robin's subjects were not likely to quarrel with him for adhering to the treaty, war being with them a second nature. They gloried in the achievements of their sovereign. Each warrior had an

African fortune, viz., several bullocks and a plurality of wives, and never calculated the chance of the slave-ship, but lived only for the day. The king was a glorious fellow in his way, and much beloved.

King Cain abided by his treaty, and fell by it.

At Cape Mount were a few traders from Liberia, who, at enormous profits, exchanged clothes and gin for rice and palm oil. One of these, a Cherokee Indian, had married a sister of Cain's; his name was Curtis, and, by the way, he was a very useful, civil man.

Running into anchorage on the 21st of July, a canoe brought the following note:—

"A revolution has taken place; King Cain is murdered; my house is robbed, and every thing belonging either to myself or the king, has been seized. From the urgent demands of the insurgents for the copy of the anti-slave-trade treaty, known to be in my possession, I infer that this revolution is in favor of the slave-trade. All your washed clothes are taken.

"A. CURTIS."

Some secret agency was evidently working, and

it did not take long to discover it. The ex-merchant had, it was said, through a brother-in-law, a citizen of Liberia, been the cause.

King Cain fancying himself safe, never went armed, although it is the custom of his countrymen to arm themselves. Ten days after our party had left Gononamarro, the king started for the Beach-town, bringing with him a quantity of rice and other articles of exchange. On reaching Turroh-Gourral he was invited to breakfast at a neighbouring town called Mambul. On his arrival, being a Mahomedan, a sheep was given him to slaughter, and while in the act, he was killed by the head-man of the town, a brother-in-law named Munmour, at the instance of an uncle named Lamney Coy. Attended only by his son, who was also killed, he fell desperately wounded, and was dragged from the town alive, his bowels trailing along the ground, and left in the bush to die. Having burnt Turroh-Gourral the insurgents proceeded to Beach-town, and robbed it, threatening Mr. Curtis's life.

Nothing could induce the head-men to choose a new king: promise after promise was made, until at last the day and time were named.

But when assembled they refused to make a choice, and one chief, Tom Levan, argued in favour of the slave-trade, declared that neither Fano-toro, Cain, nor himself, had known what they were about when they signed the treaty, and ended by saying, that what their ancestors had done must be right, and they would sell slaves. Thus from 1846 the entire stop that had been put to the trade, had in no way altered the minds of the people, for one simple reason, that a most lucrative traffic had been denied them, an ancient, and consequently to them a sacred, custom had been stopped, and nothing had been substituted.

Not long after this, the Kroomen of H.M.S. Waterwitch took a canoe at Cape Mount, with three slaves in, bound to the factories at Bassar.

At a conference at which five of the neighbouring chiefs were present under pretence of choosing a king, Lamney Coy delivered an oration on the murder of the late king, which was interpreted by Mr. Curtis. It ran as follows:—

"A law was brought to this country by your people, I did not see the law. Fano-toro and Cain saw it, and said it was a good law; to keep that law a yearly present was to be sent by your queen, and if we sold no slaves, this present was to be divided.

"The present came, and Cain kept it; we (the chiefs) would not believe it; time passed, and as we received none of it, we called a meeting at Mamboul.

"When Cain arrived there he was asked if he had received that present; on his acknowledging it, we killed him."

Moussa explained that the murder of the king was a country palaver, and it was not hard to discern that he had taken a prominent part and was revenged.

Their whole story was a fabrication.

The slave-trade was aimed at and determined upon, and the speculation was put an end to by taking the very man, who himself stated that the affair had cost him two hogsheads of tobacco, which were not thirty miles from the Cape in a slave-ship—this man was the ex-merchant, Canot.

Treaties are made in this manner: the king is dazzled into a promise by the offer of a present, on condition that he signs a treaty he scarcely can be expected to understand. Even if he does, he has no power or control over his chiefs; and unless he gives them an equivalent they will defy him, and perhaps get rid of him altogether.

The murder of Cain was a death-blow to the treaties at the North. He was a powerful usurper, placed on the throne from his warlike habits—feared and dreaded by his neighbours—besides being a clever and ambitious man.

CHAPTER VI.

SLAVE-FACTORIES.

Gallinas is the largest establishment for the sale of slaves on the northern division; besides which there are factories at the Pongus, Sherboro, Shebar, and Grand Bassar; and the line of coast to be guarded is about one hundred and fifty miles. Some of these are migratory. Thus, the Pongus was visited by a man-of-war in March, and reported clear; while in August there were again three new factories. At Shebar, and along the Kiltain coast, a distance of about sixty miles, there are stockaded barracoons for the reception of slaves, should the Gallinas be well blockaded.

In Gallinas, the chiefs still have remains of the ancient splendour acquired by the profits of the trade in former times. Huge bowls of solid silver adorn their tables; while satin and cloth of gold bedeck their jet-black bodies. The trade, by no means so lucrative, is now carried on in muskets, powder, spirits, and piece goods; and, as was the case a short time back, the chiefs, in order to obtain credit from the Spaniards (the latter being overstocked with slaves), had recourse to the threat of requiring British assistance; thus forcing the merchants to purchase, at a low price, an article already a drug in the market.

In order, some little time past, to procure slaves at a cheap rate, one of these factors (Don Paplo Crispo) hired mercenaries, and headed by one of his clerks (who was killed), "a Spaniard," waged war against his neighbours, the chiefs of surrounding countries. Any volunteer received a musket and ammunition, with a large quantity of rice; and all prisoners were bought by barter by Don Crispo. In this way he soon acquired numbers at a very cheap rate, nor does he seem inclined to slacken his warfare. Murder is common in these factories. The factor, suspicious and cowardly, notes the slightest sign; and, whether he be right or wrong, inflicts a punishment, not according to the crime, but to his own jealous nature, often flogging an unfortunate and guiltless victim to death.

It is argued, as a reason against a belief in these atrocities, that the merchant cares for his goods, and will not damage them unnecessarily. True; but of what value (in cost price) is a slave? sometimes, and not unfrequently, ten shillings, or an old musket. Then there is the cowardly weight of fear in the balance. Eye-witnesses have described these horrors, and a factor now lives in Gallinas, who, because they had visited a man-of-war, flogged to death two Kroomen, from "Picaninny Kroo." All their countrymen deserted, and a compromise at last drew back Kroomen, but from a different portion of the country. Brazilians, Portuguese, even Spaniards, fare badly amongst these factors; and, finding their way to Sierra Leone, tell horrible stories of starvation, particularly when they happen, as was the case with the crew of the Andorinha,* to be landed at Gallinas, having intended a shipment from another part of the coast. The survivors reached Sierra Leone, several having died of fever, and told fearful tales of the Gallinas. The trade goods are supplied by vessels under American,

* Captured by the Bonetta.

French, Sardinian, or other colours of nations whose governments have rendered their treaties as abstruse as possible; and as was the case with the Maid of Islay, steamer, sometimes by English vessels.* These carry rice, palavancies, arms, ammunition, spirits, piece goods, &c., and receive money in exchange, or, should the opportunity be a good one, a cargo of slaves.

The idea prevails that a factory is nothing but a wooden hut, erected at a few dollars' expense, for the reception of slaves; and that the recommendation, so constantly quoted, to burn the factories,

* The Maid of Islay was chased by H.M.S. Alert. She hoisted no colours, and made her utmost endeavours to escape, for eight hours. When near enough, she was hailed five times without an answer, but still steaming and sailing. The Alert fired into her, and she would have sunk had she not been assisted by a large party of seamen from the Alert, her own crew at the same time deserting her at the master's written application. They were transhipped to the Alert. The master and crew escaped from Sierra Leone before the vessel was tried. Notwithstanding a certainty of her having assisted the slave-trade under the British flag, she was thrown out of court, and returned to her owners, highly to the amusement of the disaffected merchants at Sierra Leone. But it was a disgrace felt by those who, being legal traders, regarded the national honour. It may be proper to state that the Chief Justice was on leave in England at the time, and that the Maid of Islay was owned by a Bremen merchant.

simply implies burning the shed, and turning the unfortunate slave to be tied in the bush.

A factory consists of several large dwelling-houses for the members, clerks, &c.; of huge stores for the reception of goods, to the amount of sometimes one or two hundred thousand pounds; of counting-houses besides, containing bills and valuable documents, once lost, not to be recovered. Should these be burnt, and the factor followed wherever he may lead, and burnt out again and again, no capital in the world could stand against such a plan. It is said that the burning of the factories before had not the desired effect, because it was not carried into effect. The loss was too great not to be redeemed, if possible; and a change in home politics undid all that the efforts of Captain Denman and others had partially effected. The native chief trusts nobody, consequently the slave-merchant must have capital for his traffic; on the other hand, the known illegality of the trade would deter any merchant from advancing his goods one mile inland. The chiefs know full well they have no flag to protect them, and that, by application and attention, they can rid their states of foreign intruders, by opening treaties with

Great Britain. On the other hand, burn all the factories; clear the coast of Africa of the very name of foreign slave-trade; make it piracy; hang the captain, or all; and unless the governments of Cuba and the Brazils enter heart and soul in the work of suppressing it, no sooner will the squadron be lessened, than the trade will be reopened with redoubled horrors. Fear appears to prevail, that, should the squadron be withdrawn, no protection would be given to the palm-oil and other trades. Why should these trades particularly require protection, unless it be from the extraordinary practices exercised in the trade? It is not the intention of the present work to do other than point out the actual state of the slave-trade. The simple fact told in Lander's "Niger," of the acts of a captain of a palm-oil vessel, would appear to be by no means exaggerated, when the most revolting acts of retaliation are commonly exercised. A friend of mine, who had the inspection of a Mr. Effenhausen's books at Sierra Leone, learned from them that natives were entrusted, in all parts of the coast, by the Bremen merchant, with large accounts; and, as he explained, they accounted for them generally with much regard to honour.

The coast of Africa, except for the suppression of the slave-trade, would require only two vessels, provided that men-of-war, to and from other stations, called on the outward and homeward voyages.

Honest and peaceable trade, supported by a high Christian mission, can alone civilize Africa, and put a stop to a trade disgraceful to mankind. But such a plan would take years to effect; evils are to be rooted out; opinions altered; nature almost to undergo a vast change: so deeply rooted are customs in Africa, that I venture on the following anecdote to elucidate them.

King Coach (*Anglice*, "Eagle"), nicknamed Robin, of Manna, lost a wife at Cape Mount; his country was then at war, and it was his intention to remove the body at some future day; in the meantime, he caused the spirit to be fed nightly.

Q. Do you believe in such nonsense (he was a Mandingo Mahomedan)?

A. The old men, when boys, said such was the custom of their country when they were boys; and the old men then said, such has been the custom before,—it is the custom. And if King Coach willed it otherwise, the people would say, "Coach loves new customs ; let us kill him before he does away with our ancient ones."

As will be shewn in another chapter, the African kings, at least in the north, are not those despots of power generally imagined ; but must themselves conform to custom, or be snuffed out like a candle.

After this long digression, it may not be too late to return to the intention of the chapter, which is to describe a slave-factory in its relation to slaves themselves.

The slave, when offered for sale, passes the same examination that a horse, or other animal, would, with regard to his soundness, &c., in wind and limb ; nor is it difficult to discover whether he has been refractory or not. If purchased, the slave is imprisoned in a barracoon, a shed made of heavy piles, driven deep into the earth, and lashed together with bamboos, thatched with palm leaves. If the barracoon be a large one, there is a centre row of piles ; along each line of piles is a chain, and at intervals of about two feet is a large neck-link, in one of which each slave is padlocked. Should this method be deemed insufficient, two, and sometimes, in cases of great strength, three, are shackled together ; the strong man being placed between two others, and heavily ironed, and often beaten half to death beforehand to ensure his being quiet. The walls of the barracoon extend from four to six feet high, and between them and the roof is an opening about four feet, for the circulation of air. The floor is planked, not from any regard to comfort to the slave, but because a small insect, being in the soil, might deteriorate the merchandise, by causing a cutaneous disease.

Night and day these barracoons are guarded by armed men: the slightest insubordination is immediately punished.

Twice a day all but the most refractory are allowed out in the frontage, for the purpose of feeding, washing, and performing other offices: after each meal they are obliged to dance for exercise.

Should the slave be shipped from the first barracoon, terrific horrors are saved; but if, on the other hand, the blockade is well kept up, hundreds of them are marched together considerable distances along the sea-coast, for more convenient places of shipment. In these marches dozens die of thirst, being whipped up to the last moment. A river is always made available, canoes being transported thither, and these chance-streams become the Lethe of Tartarus to the resuscitated slaves.

When a chance offers for shipping, they are driven into the boats, and at considerable risk are pulled on board. It not unfrequently happens, that one of these boats is capsised, and some hundreds of victims are drowned.

Sometimes, the blockade being well kept, it is impossible for the factors to load a vessel for months: the misery endured by the slave during this time, can only be imagined. Constantly marched backwards and forwards, a distance of seventy and eighty miles, from the increase of expense, and frequently from the absolute want of provision, they are half starved; or, perhaps (as was the case in 1847, to the number of 2,000), they are murdered for want of provisions to keep them.

CHAPTER VII.

SLAVE SHIPS.

EACH trade requires a particularly constructed vessel; and, from their peculiarity, those accustomed to naval affairs can at once single out a slaver from a number of vessels—(could not any one tell an Indiaman from a collier?)—for of all the ships employed in whatsoever capacity, none are more beautiful than the generality of slavers. This is a rule with many exceptions, as, from the exigencies of the trade, the merchant cannot always command capital to fit out a number of vessels, with an almost certainty of losing a large portion of them. Thus, very frequently, small and inferior vessels are equipped and sent to the coast, to act if possible as decoys, and should opportunity offer to ship and bring over a cargo of slaves. One of these, the Triumfo, was taken in May by H.M.S. Amphitrite. Her condition was as follows: Rope, scarcely any ; sails so bad, that the sailmaker of the frigate pronounced them beyond repair. She had none of the equipment for a slaver ; but could not account for herself, nor explain why she should carry a number of empty casks.

Although condemnable, she could not well be burnt, as legal condemnation before a Court was then by no means sure ; and should her owners gain a cause, damages would be heavy. Accordingly she was ordered to St. Helena, but being unable to fetch, she bore up and reached Sierra Leone ; the prize crew living on farinha and water, and the sails being patched with the bed-linen of the second master in charge of her. The captain of the Triumfo stated that a new suit of sails and rigging was ready at Lagos, where she was to ship her slaves.

The equipment of the regular slaver is attended with a large outlay, in short no expense is spared. She is run up for the voyage, and should she be found strong enough for another, she undergoes a thorough repair. In order to make her light and buoyant, her timbers and beams are small, and screwed together : when chased, these screws are loosened to give the vessel play. After the hull is built, she is placed in the hands of the coopers, who erect, in the hold, huge water-casks, called leaguers. On these are stowed the provisions, wood, &c.; above them is the slave-deck. Thirty-six inches may be considered a medium height, but they sometimes measure four feet six inches; while, on the other hand, that of the Tragos Millas* was fourteen, and of the Pharafoal eighteen inches, intended for children only. One of these hellish nurseries was taken in 1842 by H.M.S. Fantome. She measured eighteen tons, and had, besides a crew of five Spaniards, one hundred and five slaves (with one exception, a girl of fourteen), under nine and over four years of age. She had no slave deck, but the children were stowed on the casks and fire-wood in bulk: her name also was the Triumfo.

The upper deck is generally clear, except of the sweeps or oars for calms, and a covered sleeping-place, about six feet long by three feet wide on each side for the captain and pilot. Some have guns, but the system of arming is by no means common now. A felucca, taken by the boats of H.M.S. Philomel and Dart, in January 1848, had

* Two ships taken by H.M.S. Bonetta.

a long 18-pounder, with which she did great execution.

The story is as follows:—Information having been obtained, H.M.S. Rapid sighted her in light weather, and chased, by means of the yawl, which the felucca escaped.

Some days after, she was seen in a calm at daylight by H.M.S. Philomel and Dart. The Dart's boats were beaten off, but afterwards assisted the Philomel's to take her. The gun in consequence of the mizen mast could not be pointed right aft. Lieutenant, now Captain Wharton, pulled with the felucca's masts in one, right for her stern, thus precluding the possibility of an effectual discharge; notwithstanding which, from the gun being loaded with every species of combustible, and scattering, seven men were put *hors de combat* by its discharge. They singled out the captain, who was a desperate fellow, and after shooting him, they boarded and took possession.

It was said that directly the men-of-war were seen, he called his two look-out men from the mast-head and shot them.

When they carry a boat, it is a very small one, and generally serves as a hen-coop.

The rigging and sails are fitted with a sailor-like neatness not to be expected. The sails from the frequency and force of the tornadoes, are very low, and bent broad; thus, in a brig of about 140 tons taken by H.M.S. Dolphin, in May, the fore-yard was seventy-six feet, or as long as a frigate of 1000 tons would be in H.M. service. So beautifully were all her ropes racked aloft—*i.e.* tied—so that a shot cutting them, the sail would still remain set, that after a cannonade of sixty shot, in which upwards of fifty had taken effect, not one sail was lowered.

The articles by which a slaver can be condemned if found in possession of slaves, are all or either of the following:—

A slave-deck, or planks ready for a deck, slave-irons, or coppers,* an extra quantity of farinha, rice, water, or other provisions she cannot account for having.

In the regular slaver no questions need be asked. As the boarding officer ascends the side, he

* The slave coppers are a large cooking-apparatus, for the slaves and crew, standing generally amid-ships of the upper deck. There can be no mistake about them, and they could be of no possible use in a vessel having them on board, as from their size they must be inconvenient.

is generally accosted in English by the crew, requesting to know if they are to go in that boat, as each stands with his bag ready for transhipment.

The slaver generally leaves her port equipped with provisions, wood and water, for the return voyage, and for the accommodation of the crew, carries the outward passage stock on the slave deck; in this they are well found, all kinds of luxuries being frequently discovered on board at the time of capture.

The crew are formed as follows:—the captain is in the manifest a supercargo, who is perhaps not there at all, or who passes for a passenger when taken, and with an umbrella under his arm makes himself look as shore-going as he can. The salary varies, but it is seldom less (at a venture) than 250*l.* for each hundred slaves; but should the voyage not be a clear one, all demands are null, not only to the captain, but to all employed.

Should the vessel be taken, a new captain is found. This man's title is Capitano de Bandiera, or Captain of the flag. He has to take the responsibility and delay of the position, is frequently a tailor, or, as was the case in the Oppoceçao schooner, taken by H.M.S. Pearl in 1838, a grog-shop keeper, at Matazas. A clear voyage pays him from one to two hundred pounds.

The pilot's is the next situation of responsibility and pay. Of these, there are three classes; the higher is but little inferior in any way to the captain, and, as in the case of Don Pedro Bramo, he often amasses large sums. The Don was formerly a pilot, then a slave-factor, at Gallinas; and had he not ruined himself in a law-suit, against Captain Denman, might still be living in a palazzo, in Madrid. The duty of the pilot is understood by its name, and as such, he never leaves the deck. A captain, or a pilot, may each clear a thousand pounds a voyage, and it is quite possible for three voyages to be made yearly; many of both classes embark in the risk, and make large fortunes.

The boatswain is a superior class of sailor, and frequently a most useful hand. As he is one of the condemning class, great numbers of these find their way to Sierra Leone. The boatswain of the Oppoceçao, in a gale of wind in the Bay of Biscay, being one of a small crew in a merchant brig, distressed for a captain and hands, from Sierra Leone, made a jib-boom and rigged it himself, being the only man in the vessel that could do seaman-like duty. Below this man it is needless to descend; suffice it, that all the scoundrels and vagabonds, of the worst description, drawn from starvation by a lottery of wages, are here collected; and if there be one greater rascal than another, it is he, who, invariably found polite in the extreme, doffs his hat, and offers himself as interpreter. He speaks English, and will sell his brother to gain your favour.

On taking an empty slaver, all the crew, except the captain, pilot, and cook, who is considered a responsible person, are removed to the man-of-war, to be landed at the nearest and most convenient part of the coast. Having, from the Bonetta, landed two prize-crews at Gallinas, in her boats, Don Jozé Luiz wrote a most polite note, stating the inconvenience, he concluded, must arise from many ships' boats in the surf, and offering to send a boat at any time—the white flag was hoisted at the fore.

Don Luiz and the slave-factors were rid of an espionage, and the Bonetta of a great trouble. It is almost needless to remark, that the boat was always sent.

With copies of the treaties, which authorize the taking of the vessel, and a full account of the capture, an officer and a party of men, from the man-of-war, are placed on board, to navigate the prize to the port of condemnation, where she is received by the proctor, who puts the case into court, and at the end of fourteen days, if a clear case, she is condemned.

As soon as she arrives, the marshal of the court visits her and takes an inventory. She is shipped by the prize crew, and everything is prepared for the sale.

The captured vessel is termed a prize, but in reality she is an illegal trader, detained for adjudication, as was proved by the case of a prize to H.M.S. Waterwitch. The crew if they find a fitting opportunity, have a right to attempt a re-capture. At the same time the prize-officers, for the better safety of the *détenus* may put them in irons, or confine them in any way he pleases.

As soon as the vessel reaches the port of adjudication, the captor is set on shore, with an allowance of two shillings, and the others of one shilling a-day until she is condemned.

The officer having made an affidavit to the

truth of the statements, appears in court on the fourteenth day, when, unless any protest has been laid, she is declared a lawful prize to the Queen.

A sale then takes place of hull and furniture. The marshal takes the vessel in Tourol (or Destruction Bay), and having seen her sawn in two, hands her over to the purchaser.

The trade in old copper, rigging, and other furniture is considerable from these sales to the United States. Such then is the empty slaver.

But the full one in its horrors almost defies description. Judging from experience, hardly any one, however hardy he be, first puts foot over her side, but he pays a tribute to the initiation by a voluntary contribution to the finny tribe.

Arrived on the coast, and the port reached, if no man-of-war be on the spot, two hours suffice to place four hundred human beings on board. The case of the San Francisco was this. She was signalled to come in from Gallinas, and in two hours her slaves were shipped. It then fell calm, and remained so for fourteen hours, during which time (the current drifting her) the boats remained alongside ready, should a man-of-war appear, to re-land them.

In May, the steam-trader Maid of Islay, belonging to a Bremen merchant, of Sierra Leone, being engaged in landing rice for the slave-merchants of Gallinas (under the British flag), was mistaken fer a Brazilian steamer, and her crew reported that 1,200 slaves were sent alongside in six boats, but pulled on shore as soon as the mistake was discovered. These are the same boats that Don Luiz sent for the prize crews, and fully capable of holding 200 slaves each. They are rowed by forty men, whose seats are so high that a man can walk underneath.

On the slaves being received, the largest men are picked out (if not sent with bad characters) as head-men, and these, dividing the slaves into gangs, according to the size of the vessel, of from ten to twenty, keep them in order. The slave deck is divided into two unequal parts, the greater for the men, the other for women and children, and between the sexes no communication takes place during the voyage.

The stowage is managed entirely by the head-men, who take care that the largest slaves shall be farthest from the ship's side, or from any position in which their strength might avail them, to secure a larger space than their neighbours. The form of stowage is, that the poor wretch shall be seated on the hams, and the head thrust between the knees, and so close that when one moves the mass must.* In this state, nature's offices are performed, and frequently, from the maddened passions of uncivilized men, a fight ensues between parties of two nations, whose warlike habits have filled the slave-ship—alike prisoners, each to the other's ruler, and all sold to the same factor. In one instance, a brig, the Isabella II., taken by H.M.S. Sappho, in 1838, had been chased off the coast for three days, and when the hatches were opened, starvation had maddened, and assisted by a regular battle between the Akoos and Eboos, had destroyed two hundred human beings.

This state of misery works, in a measure, its own cure. Fevers and cutaneous diseases, consequent on the crowded state of the decks, carry off sometimes hundreds, and leave to the survivors at

* From the close stowage, the body becomes contracted into the deformity of the position; and some that die during the night, stiffen in a sitting posture; others, who outlive the voyage, are crippled for life, and may be seen walking about the Cuba estates scarcely more erect than the position described.

least room enough. In the West Indies, vessels taken from Africa offer a most deplorable picture, many of the slaves being in dreadful agonies, from a loathsome cutaneous disease, yclept the kras-kras. It commences like the itch, between the fingers, &c., but, unless checked, it runs into ulcers of enormous size, and,from extreme irritation, often proves fatal. Should a mutiny break out, the cowardly nature of the dastards employed at once breaks forth, frequently decimating the whole, hanging some, shooting others, and cutting and maiming just sufficient to hinder a recurrence on board, and yet not to spoil the sale of the *article*.

Sometimes fear quite overpowers the slaves, as will appear in the following account of a mutiny, given by the captain of the Curioso (prize to H.M.S. Amphitrite, in May, 1848) to Lieutenant Strickland, the prize-officer. This mutiny had occurred on a previous voyage.

The state of the vessel was this:—slaves, one hundred and ninety men; crew, captain, four whites, and a black steward. The latter managed to convey, unseen, the only four cutlasses, together with three razors, to the slaves.

At three in the morning, lying ill with the fever,

he heard the slaves breaking out of the hold. Arming himself with a knife, he rushed on deck, and meeting the negroes on a narrow part of the deck, fought until the knife broke. Seizing another, and assisted by three white men, the fourth having been killed, the combat remained undecided, until one of the white men found a loaded musket, with which he soon cleared the decks.

Daylight revealed a horrid sight. As many as sixty-seven of the slaves lay bleeding or dead; in a word, the deck was a perfect scene of carnage. All the survivors were put below, and for the rest of the voyage none allowed to appear on deck. Food and water were handed through the iron gratings of the hatchways.

The slave is fed twice a day; in order to give room, one-half are allowed on deck. At the hour of the meal, they are ranged into messes, and when all is ready, at a signal from the head-men, they commence. The food consists of either rice, calabancies (a kind of bean), or farinha (the flour of the cassada, a species of potato) boiled. As a relish to these are either salt pork, beef, fish, chillies, or palm oil, in small quantities. After each meal they are made to sing, to digest the food, and then the water is served out, the fullest nominal allowance of which is one quart each, daily, though seldom more than a pint is given. The modes of administering this necessary support of nature are various. The most extraordinary is the introduction of a tin tube to the cask, and allowing each slave to have the use of it for a certain time, whereby, it is said, a little water is made to go a great way.

Irons are seldom used on board (though all slaves are provided with them), unless after a mutiny, or if closely chased by a man-of-war; in which case the condition of the slaves becomes truly dreadful. They are all barred below, and from fear of their rising, are seldom watered until the chase be over, even though it last two and three days. During a chase, every thing that can be thought of to make the vessel sail is done, however much misery it may cost the cargo; and frequently portions of these unfortunates are cast into the sea in empty casks or small boats, trusting that the compassionate captain of the cruizer will heave his vessel to, and by the detention distance the chase. It certainly must appear inconceivable that such barbarities should be carried on, yet it is a truth, that the purchaser ships a hundred, with a certainty of losing one-fifth by the voyage, owing to the crowded state of the ships.

Though irons are seldom used in the slave ships, they are in the Barracoous, and also on the estates. Visiting a sugar plantation in 1837, in the island of Martinique, the hospital for the slaves was a most barbarous affair. An inclined plane served as a bed for all, while at the lower end was a line of stocks, in which the legs of the wretches were confined when sick.

In the Brazils it is by no means an uncommon thing to burn the vessel that has delivered a safe cargo; from the disgusting stench, even the starving would not clean her.

Clever as the men may be who command these vessels, some very odd *ruses* have been carried into effect by officers in command of dull cruizers; such as, topping the yards about; and by dressing a few men in red frocks and woollens, as a merchant vessel. Authentic instances are known of the slavers running on and being taken; others, on seeing a slaver in the offing, have run off in an opposite direction under all sail, leaving their yawl behind. The unsuspecting slaver fancying one has already sailed with a cargo, runs in and is taken; while, on the other hand, a slaver known afterwards to have seven hundred on board, finding herself at day-light too near for manœuvering, hoisted American colours, and running for the man-of-war, hailed and asked her longitude.

Owing to the great demand for slaves in the Brazils, the speculators are fitting out large steamers capable, it is said, of carrying three-thousand slaves. These vessels are armed, and two only have as yet been captured; one of these was brought into H.M. service, under the name of the Snap, her engines were all on deck. With steamers the voyage is short, so a deck cargo is generally the most extensive. The want of fuel is the great objection to these vessels. The other steamer, taken in April, 1838, appeared off the Gallinas, but being chased by the boats of the northern division, the captain wrote to Don Louis, stating his inability to attempt to ship there, as for want of fuel, he must return to the Brazils, and he would then try the south coast.

He tried the south coast, and was taken by H.M.S. Penelope.

CHAPTER VIII.

THE SLAVE-TRADE AT GALLINAS.

The African kings are born warriors, yet, strange as it may appear, we have been in the habit of thinking them the greatest cowards in the world. However strong the party may be, they never fight in the day time, and seldom in the night unless the opposite party is asleep in a town. A hand-to-hand fight they have no knowledge of. Robin once told me that the Gallinas people had taken his town; on sympathising with him, he said that his people had surrounded them and intended killing all who shewed themselves, until being reduced in numbers, the rest would run.

But he had no idea of re-taking his own town, because he knew the enemy would be vigilant and would not sleep.

A man appeared near Buddal, armed at all

points; the inhabitants came out to meet him, and asked him his business; although it was known he belonged to a town that had made war, they did not attack him.

If a fight ensues, and any of the besiegers are hit, all scamper away, and on the contrary, should any get into the town, the besieged vacate if possible.

The town once taken, the besieged close every avenue as soon as possible, and all that are found become prisoners of war, and some are retained by the warriors, the rest sold to the foreigners as slaves.*

There is no mercy whatever either shewn or expected, for it is the general custom.

The slave merchants incited wars in order to reap the benefits, and thus supply themselves cheaply.

In different parts of the coast the trade takes a run: thus, at one time Ambrig, on the south-coast,

* There is one mode of fighting called "Path War." Should the besiegers be repulsed, and the besieged follow up the victory, each of the former is provided with a small-pointed spike, which he sticks into the ground. If one of the pursuers is spiked, further pursuit is stopped.

was so strongly attempted, that H.M.S. Styx took a vessel a week for eleven weeks.

One of the principal causes of the extraordinary success of the trade is, that the right of search will not admit of an inspection of an American vessel's hold.

The plan adopted is this,—a vessel is run up in the United States and freighted to the Brazils, where a negotiation is entered into, and there she takes, as passengers to the coast, a regular crew of Brazilians; meeting the men-of-war, her papers clear her, and, watching her opportunity, two hours suffice to ship and start, and a dark night will clear the cruizers. Even though she has slaves in her, the cruizer cannot touch her if she sails under American colours. Off Annobon, an American vessel, the J. W. Huntington, was boarded by a boat from the Bonetta, with a double crew: she had, according to the consulate report, twice put into Rio de Janeiro, and had been as often cleared out for the Coast of Africa, in ballast.

Another was boarded off Gallinas. She had transferred her crew at the Havannah, and was bound from there to Cabenda; but had put into Gallinas, a distance of one thousand miles to the northward, at a time that fourteen vessels, fitted from Cuba for Gallinas, and nearly six thousand slaves were in the barracoons. She had slave-coppers, and refused an inspection of her holds. In consequence of a succession of boardings, she left Gallinas — stating for Sierra Leone — but no doubt to return when the coast was clear. As long as that blind lasts it is perfectly impossible even to check the trade. These are two instances, but hundreds more could be given. Not an officer now serving on the coast but must have known several.

Vessels under French, Sardinian, Genoese, and other colours, bring out cargoes of material, and should the vigilance of the cruizer be withdrawn, or a chase take her from her post, four or five hundred are shipped; and should the slaver be at last captured, she is under no colours, and has no papers, and is condemned, "name unknown."

Slave merchants employ boats to a distance of forty miles out at sea, to watch the cruizers, and, incredible as it may appear, yet it is no less a fact, that one of H.M. ships was actually reported to that distance daily by whale-boats.

One portion of the coast is almost as good as another for a shipment, except during the severe rains, and a line of signals is constantly kept up. Thus, a single light means that the coast is clear, and the vessel may venture in; two, that the whereabouts of the cruizer is doubtful; three lights indicate great danger, which, if it increase, is shewn by repeated flashes. Should the cruizer be off the port at the time a vessel is expected, a bonfire is lighted, and every half-hour a quantity of gunpowder is thrown on it. These flashes are seen twenty miles off, and taken advantage of. With the protection of the American flag and the correct *espionage* and line of signals constantly kept up, it is impossible for the coast to be effectually guarded.

With the northern division each vessel had a line of forty miles to guard. During the rainy season, from May to November, it is for three or four days in the week almost impossible to see four miles. Should the cruizer be at anchor off Gallinas, she remains a certain mark of her whereabouts, and the slaves are marched off ten or twenty miles up or down the coast, and there shipped in the night; while, on the other hand, should she keep under weigh while at one end of the station, shipments will be made at the other. Tell a slave captain that the squadron is to be withdrawn, he remarks that he hopes not. "No hae contrabanda, no hae contrabandista," and he tells you that, instead of the high salary he now risks, he will be paid like the povre diavolo of a captain of a merchant vessel. Spaniards, Portuguese, and Brazilians are, generally speaking, gamblers, and this is a game of chance of the most exciting character, and as such they view it.

The whole conversation of the captured captain is on the quality of the vessel he will bring over next. He cares nothing for the last voyage, further than that he has wasted so many months' time, which he attributes to "La fortuna de guerra."

All the vigilance of the revenue cruizers and coast-guard service is of no avail against the cunning of these smugglers.

Strong indeed must be the measures, that even in a slight degree can prevent the shipment of slaves.

In one instance the profit may be cent. per cent., in an other even a thousand.

Although the Bonetta was but a short time employed on the northern division, yet she had her portion of duty to perform, and how she did it, let the under-mentioned captures shew.

The first chase was so extraordinary, as will appear, in its termination, that even, describing it in the most literal manner, it must seem unlikely. However, thus it was. On the 6th of March, standing into the land, near Cape Mensurada, at about seven in the morning, a schooner appeared in sight, and from her endeavours to escape, left no doubt of the illegality of her trade. Between the land and sea breeze, which set in about eleven, it was nearly a calm, with light variable airs. The chase took advantage of this to lighten, and casks, boats, planks, everything that could be, was thrown over-board; after eleven, the run was very exciting, and the schooner making for the land: presently, she took in her studding sails, and hauled to the wind. In shore, lay at anchor a man-of-war, and in the course of a short time the chase was joined by H.M.S. Rapid, and her yawl, making now four in all. Finding the Bonetta too close on her, the schooner again bore away, and by sunset (the Rapid, a long way astern), we were both under all sail, running before the wind. She appeared almost in our grasp, when a tornado took all aback;

every rope being manned, our sail came in, and running off the land, we lost sight of our chase before eight o'clock.

At half-past nine, when all but the watch were in bed, a most severe shock was felt by all; one of the watch without orders to do so, sprang to the lead, and in answer to the question, why he did so, declared, as did the whole watch, that the ship was on shore. Some below were completely thrown out of their beds; no bottom was found, and the ship was, at least, fifteen miles from land.

It might have been the shock of an earthquake.

Could it have been the sinking hull of the lightened schooner?

On the 14th of March, a vessel, seen from the mast-head at 3 P. M., immediately tacked, and endeavoured to escape. By sunset she was discernible from the deck, and a clear moon left little difficulty in keeping her in sight all night. Every manœuvre imaginable was tried in vain, proceeding on almost every point of the compass; still, when daylight broke, the vessels were so close that, after firing three shots at the slaver, she hove to, and the Brazilian brig Dois Amigos, became the first prize, with a cargo of 408 negroes.

Bearing an important cipher despatch from Sierra Leone to Captain Monypenny at Cape Mount, on the 16th May, we were becalmed for an hour, about four miles from a brigantine. Having delivered the despatch, the Bonetta was ordered to proceed to Sierra Leone. This brigantine shipped her slaves at Gallinas, and was captured in August by H.M.S. Sealark, under the name of the San Francisco; she was returning for another cargo.

Returning from Sierra Leone, in company with H.M.S. Rapid, on the 31st of May, standing in for the land about Gargwa (having luckily lost sight of the Rapid), we chased a schooner, and in four hours brought her to, when she proved to be the Brazilian slave-schooner Phoco-foo (which means light-house): her crew had perfectly cut her to pieces; all her masts were sprung, and so much damage had been done, that a party of officers, sent on board to survey, condemned her. Having removed the crew, a train was laid, and having set fire to both ends, she scarcely touched the shore when she blew up; but continued burning nearly all night. This was a vessel fully equipped for the trade, but with no slaves on board.

On the morning of the 12th of June, owing to the prevalence of strong currents and light winds, with a heavy swell, our vessel had drifted so close to the land between Manna and Gallinas, that at four A.M. it was deemed prudent to anchor. A few hours after daylight a boat was seen pulling for Gallinas. Immediately sending one in chase, they were both soon alongside the brigantine, now under weigh, and the boat proved to be one from a slaver in the offing, sent in to make arrangements for the cargo.

By information derived from this boat's crew, it appeared that their vessel would stand out for a time, but that on a certain day she would be off little Cape Mount. Acting upon this information, we kept a sharp look-out, and on the morning of the 19th, at daylight, a schooner was in sight. —The wind being very light, by nine she was scarcely visible from the deck; so detaching Mr. Smallpage (midshipman) in the gig, after a pull of nearly fifteen miles he succeeded in capturing a schooner, claiming the protection of no flag, with all fittings necessary for the slave-trade. It was called the Tragas Millas.

The next prize was descried at daylight, on the

28th of June, having Cape Mount Bay under her lee. The captain of her preferred trying to cross the bows of the Bonetta, to the chance of being embayed; accordingly we neared each other on opposite tacks, each carrying studding-sails. Suspecting from his object that the chase was a superior sailer, a cannonade was opened upon her, and so effectually, that after four shots she hove to. The prize's crew was immediately removed, though scarcely in time: one shot had passed completely through her, and tumbling right over, she nearly capsized the boat, which was bearing the last of the crew. This vessel, the Andarimha, Brazilian, fully equipped for the slave-trade, had first put into the most southern part of the coast on the 5th of May, but was chased from thence by a steamer. On the 3rd of June she again put into Ambrig, but a second time escaped, after being chased. Finding this part of the coast too well guarded, she made a voyage of about fifteen hundred miles, and sent a boat into the Pongos to arrange the cargo again. She was chased, and running from Charybdis this time, fell upon Scylla. On the 10th of August, after a run of about seven hours, and firing three blank cartridges, a schooner, called the

Alert, became a prize. She was under no flag, and had recently been bought for Don José Luiz, the factor at Gallinas; for whom, besides a full equipment of the slave-trade, she had a quantity of wine and other articles.

On the 5th of September H.M.S. Sealark chased a schooner beyond the limits of her station, when about 3° 30′ P.M. she was descried and soon chased and taken possession of by the Bonetta. She proved to be a vessel called the Louiza, and her supercargo (who passed for one Don José Segui) was one of the most notorious slave-dealers on the coast. His name was Theodore Canot, a Florentine by birth, but American, French, or English, when either suited. If all the horrible murders said to have been committed by this miscreant are true, he must be the most atrocious of mankind. While a factor at Cape Mount, almost a hundred victims are said to have fallen to his avarice, nor were all of these negroes, but in many instances white men.

The last vessel taken on the northern division, was captured in fact by the Sealark, but virtually by the Sealark and the Bonetta.

In September, being on the passage to Sierra Leone, at noon we chased a brig; while making sail, a man fell overboard, and after lowering a boat and saving the man, we made sail again, and now observed H.M.S. Sealark in chase also.

A fine breeze added to the interest of the scene. The Sealark and chase were some distance apart on the port tack. Coming up with them, at two we tacked and opened fire at extreme range, and kept it up with shot and shell until four. At seven, after the Sealark (by change of wind to windward) opened fire, the brig wore round and hove to. She proved to be the Achilles, with a double slave-deck, equipped for the shipment of a thousand slaves, and hoisting no flag. The captain of this vessel was the same who had made the successful voyage in the San Francisco, and three out of four thousand dollars cleared by that voyage, he had laid out in the Achilles, and he now lost all.

Having given the captures, it may be as well to relate the escapes. One evening, we anchored in company with a palm-oil brig, called the Mazeppa, and the master gave us the following information:—On the 25th of June he lay at anchor off Gand Cestross: a brig hove to in the offing, but after being boarded by a canoe, stood in and shipped four hundred and fifty slaves in sight of the Mazeppa.

On the 24th of July, a brig arrived at Shebar, bearing a new factor for a place called Bendo. At the same time between four and five hundred slaves had been marched there for other vessels, which, however, had been captured. The opportunity was a good one, and though unequipped for the trade, she slipped and escaped with the whole. At Sierra Leone, in the latter end of September, one man, by name Gorney, made the following deposition:—

"My name is Gorney, and I am the domestic slave of the late chief, Charles Gorney, of Gallinas. When Captain Denman burnt the factories, my late master gave him his two sons to be taken to Sierra Leone for their education. Latterly the Spaniards have tried to decoy these boys with the intention of selling them. My visit here is to warn them. This rainy season (from May to September) the Spaniards have shipped six cargoes."

One he described from Gallinas (the San Francisco); undoubtedly a second could not but be the brig at the bar; the other four were described as having been shipped at Gargua. He was certainly right in two, perhaps so in all six.

Thus, after imagining that a good blockade had been maintained, and certainly a large number of prizes had been taken, I may safely state that, during the rainy season, two thousand slaves had been shipped from the northern division of the station, and perhaps more.

CHAPTER IX.

LIBBERIA.

The free and independent state of Liberia was first purchased from the Dahie tribe, by the American Colonization Society, in the year 1823, for the following extraordinary price, in commodities :—

1 Hd. of tobacco
1 Puncheon of Rum
50 Pieces of cloth
25 Kegs of powder
1 Box of muskets.

Shortly after they were in possession, they began to feel the oppression of their neighbours, and had to add a few light presents to the above to purchase peace. At that period the colony was small, but it has now wonderfully increased, extending from Little Cape Mount (with but small exception) to Cape Palmas, and said to contain, including the Aborigines, eighty thousand inhabitants. The emigrants are mostly free men of colour from the United States, who (says the first president, Mr. Roberts), " wearied with beating the air to advance themselves to equal immunities with the whites in that country, and tired of the oppression which weighs them down there, seriously turn their attention to Liberia as the only asylum they can flee to and be happy." Many of them are liberated slaves sent out by the Colonization Society, of which Colonel Hicks is the vice-president. These emigrants have a free passage, and are maintained by the society for six months after landing. At the expiration of that time, they are thrown upon their own resources, and many do well for themselves, while others starve, being too lazy to work.

As the colony increased, levies of duties, &c., were deemed requisite; these the British traders refused to pay, the American government, by treaty, not being allowed to colonize in Africa. The consequence was, that, considering themselves sufficiently strong, the new state determined to establish a free government, and accordingly, on the 29th of July, 1847, by a most unanimous resolution, they threw off all yoke, and declared the freedom of their country, under the title of the Republic of Liberia. They assumed the American flag, with the exception of the stars, the Liberian only having one large star in the blue jack. The president's chair was offered to, and accepted by, the former governor, J. J. Roberts, Esq., a mulatto; then a vice-president, secretary of state, board of customs, and two houses of representatives (the senate and the representatives) were constituted. Besides these, each county has its local offices of justices of peace, judge of the quarter sessions, notary, public, &c.

The military is based on the most free principle, in as much as garrison duty, or any thing but the fighting itself, is considered beneath the dignity of a soldier to perform. But such does not appear to be, in the president's opinion, the proper bearing of a soldier of the Republic. "When a number of men," says he, "are acting together in a body, if one falls back to load while another advances himself to fire, the consequences of such interferences will be, as has always been found to be, that they will wound and destroy more of one another than the enemy. It is therefore absolutely necessary that the militia learn to load and fire at the same time, or as nearly together as possible, &c." They are allowed to purchase their own uniforms and keep themselves, except when actually in action After the action or service is over, they are rewarded, sometimes by a grant of money, at others by a public dinner. The title of honourable is assumed by nearly all civilians in office, and military rank by the military. Thus, every man of any pretensions in the Republic is either the Hon. Hillary Teague, &c., or Colonel Capon, General, &c.

The Republic supports two public journals; one, the "Liberia Herald," contains a good deal of foreign intelligence, besides local news.

Reader, it will be but of little consequence, if, in your ignorance, you should acknowledge that you never heard of the Republic of Liberia. But of that opinion is not the editor of the above-named paper, who thus writes, speaking of the independence of the State:—"The present crisis, I deem the most important in all of our history. The eyes of all Europe and America are upon us, and while some regard us with envy, hatred, and jealousy, others there be of nobler origin, who stand amazed at the phenomena, and admire the unparalleled improvement of our little colony, eulogise our feeble efforts, and cheer us on our tedious way."

The other journal is "Africa's Luminary," published for the Missionary Society of the Methodist Episcopal Church, and it is the organ of the Government. It is a religious paper, and supplies but little foreign news, beyond missionary correspondence.

The principal exports from Liberia are palm-oil, camwood, and ivory; but, besides these gifts of nature, the inhabitants have a great quantity of land under cultivation. In order the better to illustrate this, I may venture to give an extract of a letter from the Hon. S. A. Benson, judge of the quarter sessions of Grand Bassa County:—"We are getting on pretty handsomely with our farms. Mine has amply rewarded me this year, besides affording provender for fifty or sixty mouths; I have sold, in eatables alone, 600 dollars, the greater part to men-of-war; and the same land on which I raised these vegetables (say twenty-five acres) I have coffee regularly set out, twelve and fourteen feet apart. I appreciate my farming operations more than all my commercial business."

They scarcely grow rice sufficent to support them, and thus a trifling trade is opened with Cape Mount and the neighbouring countries.

The country craft are few, and one small vessel of one hundred and twenty tons was purchased a short time back, by the acting president, as a revenue cruizer. This infant republic cannot fail to do good, and, by setting an example of industry, may do more towards reducing the slave-trade than all the blockades.

CONCLUSION.

The coast of Africa is (and, doubtless, with good reason) looked upon with great horror by members of public services, whose turn of duty may take them there. This horror must necessarily be confined, in a great measure, to the north coast, or that part lying between Sierra Leone and Cape Palmas; for, to the south, it is comparatively healthy, while the northward of Sierra Leone, although far worse, is seldom visited. Formerly deaths were much more frequent in H.M. squadron, from the boats of the cruizers being detached on service up the rivers, and in shore during heavy falls of rain. These boats would return, after a month's absence, with scarcely a man who had not contracted the fever. This style of service is, happily, done away with (on most parts where danger is to be dreaded); and now no commander dares send a boat from his vessel to be absent during the night, without being able sufficiently to explain his reasons, which he has to state in writing to the commander-in-chief.

Another happy improvement has been made. A condemned slaver, purchased into the service, commanded by a lieutenant as tender to the senior officer's ship of the northern division, is stationed in the Sherboro river looking out for slavers. Immediately a captured vessel enters Sierra Leone, it is the duty of the proctor to send and apprize the commander of the tender, who, making the best of his way, receives on board all but the officer in charge of the prize and one man. The tender resumes her station, and every now and then communicates with the senior officer. Formerly, officers and men were left at Sierra Leone; the prize condemned, they went into lodgings on shore, and generally took fever, which often proved fatal.

The seasons are unequally divided: from May to December may be called the rainy season, though the rains abate at the end of September; and from December to May the dry season commences. During the rains the climate is cool, and comparatively healthy, although the damps are productive of ague, colds, and rheumatism. When the rains abate, the power of the sun on the moistened ground has the effect of raising heavy fogs, called smokes (from their appearance), which being inhaled, are very injurious and productive of fever. This is the trying time; and, however careful a man may be, he is not safe. As the rains abate, the weather becomes intensely hot, while once or twice a week a tornado, with terrific rain, thunder, and lightning, clears and cools the atmosphere.

These tornadoes are not in the least to be feared; they give ample warning, and invariably blow off the land. The general practice is to furl everything, and send every one below, except the officers of the watch, the man at the helm, and a Krooman to look out, and to cover over the hatchways. They rise heavily over the land, with very vivid lightning, which expands into an arch. A calm ensues for some minutes, when down comes the tornado. It is seldom that any damage is done, except perhaps in chase.

During the rains the rivers send forth such quantities of water, as to render the tides extremely strong, which, contrary to the accounts given, run to the north-west, and at seldom less than two miles an hour. At the same time, the rollers set in so heavily, together with strong south-west breezes, that it is necessary, if at anchor, to leave two anchors down to be safe ; while, if under weigh, the topsails require a double reef. The calms of the coast of Africa are not known during the rainy season.

In the hot season, the Hamathan winds blow at times pretty strong. The current takes its direction from the south-west, and runs strong in shore. But little danger need be anticipated, as the soundings are very regular, and the roll of the surf may be seen and heard, two miles distant, on a dark night.

Society must be entirely given up by those serving in the blockade. At Sierra Leone and Ascension there are a few ladies, but it is not often you pay a visit to either. Both places having their drawbacks, they are seldom sought ; while, to St. Helena, if possible, each vessel pays a yearly visit ; but some are so unfortunate as never to go there. The latter is the only place at which the seaman can land, for leave of absence—hence, a trip there is much longed for.

During the six months' service, in the rainy season, H.M.S. Bonetta lost one by fever (a young officer who, having condemned a prize at Sierra Leone, had to take lodgings on shore), and she had only four patients with fever, all of whom had been exposed on shore.

Unless there be exposure on shore, or in boat-service, it does not appear that many cases of fever ever happen, and the service now done, without endangering the lives of the crews, is, in every way, equal to what it was formerly. This saving of life may be attributed to the care taken by the present commander-in-chief, and the good order of his squadron.

APPENDIX No. I.

NUMERALS OF FOUR LANGUAGES.

	THE VAHIE.	THE GRUNOO.
1.	Dundoo	Goonoo
2.	Fillah	Tierla
3.	Saquar	Tarley
4.	Narnee	Teenah
5.	Sooloo	Noonoo
6.	Sundundoo	Dia Goonoo
7.	Sunfillah	Dia Tierla
8.	Sun Saqua	Dia Tarley
9.	Sunnanee	Dia Teenah
10.	Tang	Zehiar
11.	Tank doondw	Zehiar Goonu
20.	Mo bandy	Byacoona
21.	Mo bandy ako Doondw	Byacoona Goona
30.	Mo bandy ako Tang	"
40.	Mo Fillar bandy	"
50.	Mo Fillar bandy ako Tang	"
60.	Mo Saqua bandy	"
70.	Mo Saqua bandy ako Tang	"
80.	Mo narnee bandy	"
90.	Mo narnee bandy ako Tang	"
100.	Huna Dundw	"

	THE KROO.	THE FISHMEN.
1.	Doo	Doo
2.	Song	Song
3.	Tah	Tah
4.	Neear	Eh
5.	Moo	Djmoo
6.	Muniadu	Neeroo
7.	Muni a Song	Me Song
8.	Muni a Tah	Beoh biah
9.	Supah dul	Chie roo
10.	Poueh	Poh
11.	Poueh nado	Poh la doo
20.	Ooro	Ya ooro
21.	Ooro na doo	Ooro na doo
30.	Ooro na poueh	Ooro na Poh
40.	Ooro Song	Ooro Song
50.	Ooro Song na Poueh	Ooro Song na Poh
60.	Ooro Tah	Ooro Tah
70.	Ooro Tah na Poueh	Ooro Tah na Poh
80.	Oooro neah	Ooro eh
90.	Ooro neah na Poueh	Ooro eh na Poh
100.	Ooro moo	Ooro moo

Thus, in counting after five, six is five and one, seven, five and two, &c.; thirty, is twenty and ten added; fifty, forty and ten added; while thirty-one would be "Mo bandy ako Tango doondu," twenty added eleven. Beyond a hundred they seldom count.

APPENDIX No. II.

A vocabulary of the Vahie language, the language spoken at Cape Mount, arranged solely for this work, by the author.

World	Duñah
Heaven	Algenero
Sea	Quāi
Sun	Tai lā
Moon	Kai lo
Star	Tŏrō māro
Light	Du marja
Dark	Toong boh
Sunrise	Taila-boh
Sunset	Taila-sar
Heat	Pandee
Cold	Kiemar

ELEMENTS.

Fire	Sāh
Smoke	Se-Se
Earth	Dunah
Water	Gee
East	Tailah-boh
West	Taila-sar

SENSES.

See	Eal-jag
Hear	Eah
Smell	Eh-Quenia
Feel	Eh-boro-sorarah

FORM AND INCIDENTS TO MAN.

Shape	Saw-Kel-eh
Face	Tarro
Hands	Boroo
Deaf	Ah-willicoh-rodang
Dumb	Mumu
Blind	Ah-willimohjag
Fool	Coo-loo-yah
Mad	Boghrooh
Lame	Mang boh
Fever	Mane paude
Wound	Poah

RELATIONS IN LIFE.

Husband	Nah-Ki
Wife	Nah-musa
Father	Imfah
Mother	Imbah
Brother	Niemo
Sister	Dongmusa
Son	Nah-ding-Koom
Daughter	Nah-ding-musuman

BUILDING A HOUSE, ETC.

Wood	Sorr
Thatch	Sandah
House	King
Door	King daroo
Room	Roomaroo

FURNITURE.

Table	Mosar
Bed	Behle
Bedstead	Pingboh
Seat	Cenah
Mat	Walah

ARMS.

Spear	Tambah
Sword	Far-sah-loh
Musket	Boo
Powder	Boo-fung
Cannon	Duh-bah

ANIMALS.

Bullock	Nee
Horse	Soor
Cow	Nee musuman
Sheep	Bahwahlah
Goat	Baah
Deer	Kailah
Wild hog	Fillaro corneoh
Leopard	Kolee
Elephant	Coo mah

REPTILES.

Boa-constrictor	Meele-nah
Centipede	Pella-kah
Snake	Kah

INSECTS.

Fly	Saysa
Musquito	Sulesule
Bee	Cumeah
Ant	Dedemesa

BIRDS.

Eagle	Quaranga
Snipe	Poormarsembar
Dove	Peling
Wild duck	Horlo-koko
Duck	Poorocoнde
Fowl	Teah

METALS.

Gold	Kanee jaree
Brass	Banbog-telah
Silver	Kanee-Peghmar
Iron	Cundu
Tin	Keeng-keeng

OF A TREE.

Tree	Koom
Bark	Konforo
Bough	Koomboro
Leaf	Iamboh
Charcoal	Keembee

FRUITS.

Orange	Dumbulo
Pineapple	Kafa
Plantain	Banoh
Banana	Poroh-Banoh
Cocoanut	Poroh conjoh
Guava	Poroh puloh

VEGETABLES.

Yams	Cenah-bille
Cassada	Bassae
Sweet potatoes	Toee
Ground nuts	Gendele
Onions	Ceboloh
Chillies	Kalafae
Beans	Sor
Sugar cane	Pameg

SPICES.

Salt	Corr
Pepper, cayenne	Poroh Kalafae
Oil	Turu

EATABLES, ETC.

Meat	Swea
Palm-wine	Joe-pegh
Spirits	Poroh-pegh
Flour	Baffu-fumee
Bread	Boffu
Fish	Neoh
Beef	Nea-swea
Pork	Cornea-swea

TIMES AND SEASONS.

Year	Sang
Month	Koloo
Morning	Sammah
Evening	Jeremah-silo
Noon	Sillo-cunu-teh
Midnight	Sim-teh
To-day	Wah-teh
To-morrow	Sinoh
Yesterday	Cunnu
End	Ah-dah
Beginning	Cunnith-beuah

ADJECTIVES.

Able	Koondah
Acid	Dooroh
Acute	Blāzee
Aged	Kaun-galah
Agreeable	Koh-neih
Alike	Neah-bee
Alive	Ken-deh
Bad	Man-yea
Barren	Fuemar
Bent	Dun-lah
Black	Femah
Boiling	Wuhlee

Brave	Tahpeh-lee
Bright	Marlah
Broad	Booh-ko-loh
Broken	Ah-ko-lee
Careful	Koo-ma-felleh
Cheap	Songah-ma-felleh
Clean	Koh-loe
Clever	Koh-sah
Cloudy	Bandah beelah
Coarse	Tank-koloh
Complete	Koon leendey
Crooked	Dūdūlah
Daily	Lor begh
Dead	Ah far
Dear	Songor-koh-koh
Deep	Mar-ke-lee
Disobedient	Toroh-pegh-leh
Distant	Kang-poong
Drunk	Pegh-belah
Drey	Ahpah-rah
Easy	Pĭh
Empty	Foloh
Enough	Ahcundah
Equal	Kaun dah
False	Paun goh
Fat	Too,—roh-ah
Female	Muh su
Few	Mah feu fah
First	Sinjal
Fit	Acundah-ping
Free	Manjah-din
Future	Jae loh
Glad	Vouyee
Great	Songor-billeh
Guilty	Ah-paist-muh

Hard	Pih-leigh
Heavy	Frurah
High	Condo jaug
Hot	Pandee-ah
Hungry	Kong-ah
Jealous	Musu fallah
Ignorant	Ku-luh-yah
Improper	Amar
Just	To nau
Laborious	Poh-ro-wellytoo
Large	Ko-loh
Last	Pie-nae-mae
Late	Eah-fegh-gou-gau
Less	Lun-mah-Ko-loh
Long	Ah-faug
Loose	Jong-jong
Lost	Ah-sain-ah
Mole	Ki
Middle	Teh-ma
More	Boroh
Near	Fauh
New	Nain-ah
Next	Ah-manĕā
Numerous	Con-lum bah
Old	Coroh-coroh
Open	E-dah-kol
Pale	Pu-oo
Past	Ah billy
Perfect	Ah-pegh-leh mal
Plain	Ko-main
Poor { in flesh	Toroh
Poor { in pocket	Tanah
Pretty	Au-nae-pah
Quick	Deah-deah
Rapid	Ah-pahlu-dele-bah
Red	jarrah

Rough	Quan-quan
Same	Ah-Tarro
Savage	Filau mooh
Short	Cundu
Sick	Kelah
Slow	Deah
Soft	Pau-lee
Sorry	Porro-Turroh
Strong	Gah-nah
Sweet	Kin-rah
Thick	Digbe-digbe
Thirsty	Gee-kellee
Timid	Mele-maih
True	Mar-kang
Unequal	To naih-muh
Unwilling	Mar-dou
Useful	D'he
Useless	Co-foro
Warm	Tomu-tomu
Wrong	Ah-mai
Yellow	Swaugh

PRONOUNS AND CONJUNCTIONS.

I	Eh-gar
Thou	E-war
He	Ki-mal
We	Muh-beigh
You	E-wah
They	Mo-mal-nou
Who	Jauh
Which	Ah-menah
My	En-tah
His	Ah-tah-mu
Ours	Muh-tah-mu
Yours	Eh-wah-lah-mu
Theirs	Ah-nou-tah-mu

Each	Kih-oh-keh
All	Pĭ-leh
Either	Kae-au-kae
Neither	Ah-dondo-Pelloh
This	Kae
That	Kae-nae
Some	Boro
Other	Ah-ro-maudee
Such	Kae-tohro

VERBS.

Abuse	Bellah-jouh
Accept	Kae-bellah
Accuse	Co-cee
Answer	A-er
Arrive	Ah-kae
Ask	Eh-tusuh
Assist	Eh-bassararah
Bargain	Longsh-ce
Beat	Belly-ah-rah
Beg	Fuleh-key
Begin	Kroo-bee
Believe	E-sararah
Bind	Ko-killeh
Bite	Keing
Boil	Eh-tah-ah-tah
Bring	Eh-nar-ah
Buy	Eh-sang
Call	Eh-killee
Carry	Eh-tarra
Chew	Dong
Collect	Dah-saug
Come	Eh-nah
Count	Eh-daunt
Cut	Teah
Dance	Dong-Kaeh

Deliver	Eh-cor
Destroy	Ah-lah-jauh
Die	Ab-Fah-la-muh
Divide	Teh-dung
Double	Eh-ce-nau-mal
Dress	Mar-kille
Drunk	Eh-mee
Eat	Fing-dong
End	Ah-daugah
Explain	Ero-jay-roh
Enter	Eh-dong
Invite	Kae-em-borah
Kick	Seng
Kill	Eh-foh
Kiss	Eh-dah-saw-nouh-roh
Know	Nah saw
Laugh	Jelle-kae
Lend	Lingar
Lie	Fanier
Live	Fillar-boh
Look	Ehu-fillar
Love	Deah
Make	Eueah
Mend	Ero-heah
Move	Sach-noo
Neglect	Nquien-ah
Obey	Colch-deng
Occupy	Benow
Open	Eh-doeh-Kah
Offer	Eoh
Owe	Pavyh
Paddle	Eh-woolleh
Part	Eh-Teh-Koh
Pay	Pagwah-Ka
Please	Ko-neh

Prepare	Eh-mar-kelle-nquear
Promise	Cul-leh-bih-lah
Protect	Cum-mah-fillah
Quarrel	Quah-lee
Receive	Ah-Kal-hu-bordh
Recollect	Ah-Beh-in-condo
Rob	Kounbah
Run	Boole-kal
Sail	Fillah-Kal
Stay	En-doh
Sell	Kau
Sing	Dong-boh
Sleep	Kee-Keh
Speak	Eh-for
Stab	Eh-sor-meaha
Stop	Sor
Swear	Bohoh-Kal
Take	Ebee
Talk	Dec-um-bo
Tell	Imbah-a-forwar
Tear	Tal
Think	Condor-Keller-mar
Tremble	Manee-Sambah
Trust	Eh Sahe-roh
Understand	Nah san
Wake	Cer-mae
Walk	Tah-eah
Watch	Eh-mah-ke-kal
Want	Em-woo-ah-rah
Weep	Dee-kal
Weigh	Sumar
Wish	Eh wooroh
Work	Sor-Kelv

APPENDIX No. III.

The number of slaves shipped in 1768, from Africa, for America and the islands, according to Parliamentary Reports, was 97,000.

Of these, French	23,000
Dutch	11,000
Portuguese	1,700
English	60,000
Of these latter the British Colonies received	22,000
Virginia	7,000
Shipped in British bottoms to Portuguese and Spanish Colonies	38,000

APPENDIX No. IV.

A list of the average number of slaves, supposed to have been taken from Africa, yearly; from Parliamentary Reports.

1805 to 1810	85,000
1810 to 1820	80,000
1820 to 1825	70,000
1825 to 1830	94,000

1830 to 1835 58,000
1835 to 1840 101,000
To the Brazils ... 65,000
Cuba...... 29,000

1840 to 1845 32,000
In 1846 64,000
1847 60,000
The Brazils ... 58,000
Cuba 2,000

APPENDIX No. V.

The number of vessels adjudicated upon, by the courts of Sierra Leone, Rio, Surinam, and Loando, with the number of slaves emancipated, between 1819 and 1845. From the Parliamentary Reports.

Sierra Leone—
Adjudicated 527
Condemned 501
Rio de Janeiro
Condemned 49
Surinam
Condemned............... 1
Loando
Condemned 14
Slaves Emancipated 103,191

APPENDIX No. VI.

Table, shewing the decrease of slaves imported into the Spanish colonies; from Parliamentary Reports.

1788				25,000
1788	to	1805	average	15,000
1805	„	1810	„	30,000
1810	„	1815	„	30,000
1815	„	1820	„	32,000
1820	„	1825	„	39,000
1825	„	1830	„	40,000
1830	„	1835	„	40,000
1835	„	1840	„	29,000
1840	„	1845	„	7,000
		1846		1,500
		1847		2,000

APPENDIX No. VII.

Table, shewing the increase of importations into the Brazils.

PORTUGUESE.

1788	18,000
1788 to 1805	20,000
1805 to 1810	25,000
1815 to 1820	33,000
1820 to 1825	37,000

THE BRAZILS.

1825 to 1830	50,000
1830 to 1835	15,000
1835 to 1840	65,000
1840 to 1845	22,000
1846	60,000
1847	60,000

APPENDIX No. VIII.

Table, shewing the prices given for a slave, at different periods, in the Brazils.

1784		175	dollars.
1788	from 220 to	250	"
Up to 1830	average	200	"
1830		300	"
1831		175	"
1835		300	"
1840		375	"
1843	from 325 to	175	"
1844		300	"
1845		275	"
1846		500	"
1847		250	"

THE END.